The Constraints-Led Approach

For the last 25 years, a constraints-based framework has helped to inform the way that many sport scientists seek to understand performance, learning design and the development of expertise and talent in sport. *The Constraints-Led Approach: Principles for Sports Coaching and Practice Design* provides students and practitioners with the theoretical knowledge required to implement constraints-led approaches in their work.

Seeking to bridge the divide between theory and practice, the book sets out an 'environment design framework', including practical tools and guidance for the application of the framework in coaching and skill acquisition settings. It includes chapters on constraints-led approaches in golf, athletics and hockey, and provides applied reading for undergraduate and postgraduate students of motor learning, skill acquisition and developing sport expertise.

Providing a thorough grounding in the theory behind constraints-led approaches to skill acquisition, and a foundational cornerstone in the Routledge Studies in Constraints-Based Methodologies in Sport series, this is a vital pedagogical resource for students and practising sports coaches, physical education teachers and sport scientists alike.

Ian Renshaw is an Associate Professor in the School of Exercise and Nutrition Sciences at Queensland University of Technology, Brisbane, Australia. Ian has worked in the higher education sector since 1990 delivering courses to undergraduate students and supervising postgraduate students in the UK, New Zealand and Australia. Ian has collaborated with Cricket Australia Centre of Excellence, Queensland Academy of Sport, Australian Institute of Sport and was a founder member of the Australasian Skill Acquisition Research Group.

Keith Davids is Professor of Motor Learning at the Centre for Sports Engineering Research, Sheffield Hallam University, UK. He has held professorial positions in the UK, New Zealand, Australia and Finland (Finnish Distinguished Professor 2012–2016). He has conducted research on elite and developmental sport programmes at the New Zealand South Island Academy, the Queensland Academy of Sport, Australian Institute of Sport, Diving Australia, Cricket Australia and the English Institute of Sport.

Daniel Newcombe is a Senior Lecturer in Sport, Coaching and PE in the department of Sport, Health Sciences and Social Work at Oxford Brookes University, UK. Daniel has worked in higher education for ten years and has been delivering Coaching: Practice to Theory modules to undergraduate students. Daniel is also an international and domestic national league hockey coach. He has been the assistant coach for the Men's Welsh National Team for the past seven years.

Will Roberts is a Senior Lecturer in Sport and Exercise Science in the School for Sport and Exercise, University of Gloucestershire, UK. Will has worked in higher education for the last 15 years and held academic teaching positions for over a decade in elite sport environments, establishing his work as a multi-disciplinarian in sport coaching research. Will developed the undergraduate and postgraduate research programmes in coaching at Oxford Brookes University, where he holds a post as visiting researcher in the Centre for Movement, Occupational and Rehabilitation Sciences (MOReS).

Routledge Studies in Constraints-Led Methodologies in Sport

A constraints-led framework has informed the way that many sport scientists seek to understand performance, learning design and the development of expertise and talent in sport, but its translation from theory to everyday coaching practice has proven challenging. *Routledge Studies in Constraints-Based Methodologies in Sport* provides practitioners and academics with material relating to the full breadth of the application of a constraints-based methodology in sport to in order to bridge this gap.

Introduced by a foundational text which sets out a practical design framework, and including concise books on sport-specific studies written by expert coaches, the series includes content on motor learning, skill acquisition and talent development for undergraduate and postgraduate students, and specialist knowledge on different constraints-led models for coaches, physical education teachers, sport scientists and performance analysts.

The series provides the most comprehensive, theoretically sound and practically relevant guide to understanding and implementing constraints-led approaches to skill acquisition and talent development.

Series Editors: Ian Renshaw, Queensland University of Technology, Australia

Keith Davids, Sheffield Hallam University, UK

Daniel Newcombe, Oxford Brookes University, UK

Will Roberts, University of Gloucestershire, UK

The Constraints-Led Approach
Principles for Sports Coaching and Practice Design
Ian Renshaw, Keith Davids, Daniel Newcombe, and Will Roberts

For more information about this series, please visit: https://www.routledge.com/sport/series/RSCBMS

The Constraints-Led Approach

Principles for Sports Coaching and
Practice Design

Ian Renshaw, Keith Davids,
Daniel Newcombe and
Will Roberts

Routledge
Taylor & Francis Group

LONDON AND NEW YORK

First published 2019
by Routledge
2 Park Square, Milton Park, Abingdon, Oxon OX14 4RN

and by Routledge
52 Vanderbilt Avenue, New York, NY 10017

Routledge is an imprint of the Taylor & Francis Group, an informa business

British Library Cataloguing-in-Publication Data
A catalogue record for this book is available from the British Library

Library of Congress Cataloging-in-Publication Data
Names: Renshaw, Ian, author. | Davids, K. (Keith), 1953- author. |
  Newcombe, Daniel (Daniel J.), author. | Roberts, Will
  (William M.), author.
Title: The constraints led approach principles for sports coaching
  and practice design / Ian Renshaw, Keith Davids, Daniel Newcombe,
  Will Roberts.
Description: Abingdon, Oxon ; New York, NY : Routledge, 2019. | Series:
  Routledge studies in constraints-based methodologies in sport | Includes
  bibliographical references.
Identifiers: LCCN 2018046833| ISBN 9781138104068 (hardback) | ISBN
  9781138104075 (pbk.) | ISBN 9781315102351 (ebook)
Subjects: LCSH: Coaching (Athletics) | Physical education and training. |
  Sports sciences.
Classification: LCC GV711 .R46 2019 | DDC 796.07/7—dc23
LC record available at https://lccn.loc.gov/2018046833

ISBN: 978-1-138-10406-8 (hbk)
ISBN: 978-1-138-10407-5 (pbk)
ISBN: 978-1-315-10235-1 (ebk)

Typeset in Sabon
by Swales & Willis Ltd, Exeter, Devon, UK

Printed and bound in Great Britain by
TJ International Ltd, Padstow, Cornwall

Ian Renshaw: I dedicate this book to all those teachers and coaches who selflessly give so much of themselves to others.

Keith Davids: Thanks to all the sports practitioners who have adopted an ecological dynamics rationale to underpin their constraints-based approach. A special thanks to all those who have shared, and who continue to develop and share, their most invaluable experiential knowledge. Your input and open minds are invaluable and a source of inspiration as we seek ways to help individuals realise their potential, improving the learning experiences of athletes at all performance levels.

Danny Newcombe: I would like to thank all of the coaches, players, coach developers and academics who I have been lucky enough to learn and develop with. Long may the conversations continue.

Will Roberts: Thank you to all the academics, coaches, athletes and students that have been, and continue to be, the cornerstone of my own learning journey. I have been fortunate to have been inspired, influenced, challenged and supported by you all.

Contents

Figures

Tables

Preface

A constraints-based framework has informed the way that many sport scientists seek to understand performance, learning design and the development of expertise and talent in sport, but its translation from theory to everyday coaching practice has proven challenging. *Routledge Studies in Constraints-Led Methodologies in Sport* provides practitioners and academics with material relating to the full breadth of the application of a constraints-based methodology in sport in order to bridge this gap.

Introduced by this foundational text, which sets out a practical design framework, and including concise books on sport-specific studies written by expert coaches, the series includes content on motor learning, skill acquisition and talent development for undergraduate and postgraduate students, and specialist knowledge on different constraints-based models for coaches, physical education teachers, sport scientists and performance analysts.

The series provides the most comprehensive, theoretically sound and practically relevant guide to understanding and implementing constraints-led approaches to skill acquisition and talent development.

Acknowledgements

We would like to thank the many coaches, sport scientists, teachers and practitioners that have helped to shape our thoughts on Constraints based methodologies in sport. Particular thanks must go to Peter Arnott and Graeme McDowall for their contributions to the practical chapter on coaching golf, and to Matt Wood and his athletes for their insights and expertise in developing the Track and Field chapter. Finally, to Ben Stafford and Ben Franks, many thanks for your contributions in the proofing stages of this book.

1 Introduction

Since 1994, a constraints-led framework, predicated on an ecological dynamics theory, incorporating key ideas from ecological psychology, dynamical systems theory, evolutionary biology and the complexity sciences, has informed the way that many sport and coaching scientists seek to understand performance, learning design and the development of expertise and talent in sport. This research programme has contributed to an understanding of performance, learning and talent development through an integration of theory, modelling, empirical data collection and applications in practice. Indeed, it has been argued that the constraints-led framework could provide a Grand Unified Theory to explain how athletes function during sport performance (Glazier, 2015).

Over the past two decades, application of the constraints-led framework to performance, learning and athlete development in sport has prioritised a number of strategical aims. First came the theoretical development of the framework (e.g. Araújo & Davids, 2011b; Davids et al., 1994; Davids et al., 2006; Passos, Araújo, & Davids, 2016; Seifert et al., 2014; Williams et al., 1999). Next, its application in understanding learning design for skill acquisition (e.g. Araújo et al., 2009; Davids et al., 2008; Handford et al., 1997; Savelsbergh et al., 2003; Pinder et al., 2011; Renshaw et al., 2010), and enhancing expertise and developing talent in sport (e.g. Araújo, & Davids, 2011a; Passos, Davids, & Chow, 2016; Renshaw et al., 2012), was prioritised. As with any dynamic theoretical framework for practitioners in sport, these scientific and theoretical tasks are emergent, continuous and overlapping.

An important current feature of the contribution of the constraints-led framework for understanding skill, expertise and talent development, is a focus on enhancing the *quality* of practice in developmental and elite sport (Chow et al., 2016). This process emphasises the important contribution of coaches and teachers in applying constraints-led methodologies in their practical work. An important challenge is to tap into evidence from the *experiential knowledge* of experienced practitioners and athletes involved with elite and developmental sport performance programmes (e.g. Burnie et al., 2018; Greenwood et al., 2012; Greenwood et al., 2014; Phillips et al., 2010). A constraints-led framework is founded on a rich integration between theory, science and knowledge from high-quality, applied practice in sport. Enhancing and advancing constraints-led pedagogy is, therefore, a symbiotic process where academics and researchers and practitioners can co-create new knowledge and understanding.

The limited amount of research undertaken in this current phase has revealed excellence in innovative and creative sport practice and training programmes around the world. Constraints-Led coaching is enjoying significant attention from the sporting world and is beginning to impact athlete development and practice at the elite level across sports including golf, swimming, cricket, figure skating, cycling, Paralympic sport and team sports like rugby union and association football. However, there are currently no *sport-specific* coaching/sport pedagogy/sport scientist books that have adopted a constraints-led methodology. This series of books seeks to fill this void by giving a voice to those expert practitioners who are willing to share their evidence-based practice in order to improve the quality of practical and applied work in sport from recreational, through developmental, to elite performance levels. An additional goal is to support the development of nonlinear pedagogy through the provision of practical exemplars that will enable readers to understand how the key principles of ecological dynamics (i.e. the theory) underpin current practice in a variety of sports. For readers new to the area, a clarification of the relationships between ecological dynamics, nonlinear pedagogy (NLP) and the constraints-led approach (CLA) might be of some value at this point. Ecological dynamics describes the theory that supports the NLP framework. Nonlinear pedagogy refers to the pedagogical principles that underpin the constraint-led approach, which is the methodology of manipulating constraints during practice task designs. Specifically, the books in the series can provide practitioners, working at different levels in sport, from recreational through developmental to elite performance programmes across the world, with dedicated materials on the application of a constraints-led methodology in sport. The books will be of interest to sport scientists, coaches, teachers, trainers, performance analysts, rehabilitation therapists and academics (staff and students in sport science, physical education, coaching science, performance analysis and sports engineering).

An overview of the book series

The book series will consist of an initial foundation text followed by a series of sport-specific books. The foundation text will present key ideas from the theoretical background of ecological dynamics and a *4-Principle Model* for implementing a constraints-led methodology in a principled framework to support the sport-specific texts that will follow in the series. The foundation text will ensure that readers are brought up to date with a current integration of theory, science and practice in ecological dynamics, and discuss principles of practice application using examples from several sports in a general presentation framework. The book is targeted at practitioners and academics, generally, to provide them with a sound fundamental understanding of the importance of founding learning design on sound theoretical principles. The sport-specific books in the series will have a distinct emphasis on practice and training design, making them an accessible and practical resource intended to inspire critical reflection, continuous theoretical consideration and methodological innovation by practitioners.

Subsequent books in the series will focus on specific sports and aim to provide up-to-date content by selected, leading practitioners (working at elite and developmental levels in different sports) who currently use different aspects of a constraints-led methodology in their work. A key aim will be to illustrate how practice and training design is used in their methodology. Authors will use an evidence-based approach, highlighting practical examples, personal experiences, anecdotes, statistical data and qualitative information to exemplify sound practice in a specific sport. Case studies will be to the fore to elucidate the way that the expert practitioners are applying the ideas of ecological dynamics in their work. Each sport-specific book in the series will start with a series of chapters discussing the practice of the author, illustrating examples from his/her work for readers. Each book will conclude with an explanatory chapter by the specific practitioner(s), co-authored with the series editors (Ian Renshaw, Keith Davids, Danny Newcombe and Will Roberts) to explain how the theoretical principles of the constraints-led methodology have been applied in the context of the specific sport highlighted in the text. The books will include: (i) undergraduate content on motor learning, skill acquisition and expertise and talent development in sport, (ii) similar post-graduate content for dissertations, and (iii), specialist knowledge on different types of constraints-led pedagogical activities for coaches, teachers, sport science support staff and performance analysts.

Each book will provide academics and students of sport science, coaching science, physical education and performance analysis courses with reference material that can direct studies to support learning and education. Throughout the book series it will be emphasised that readers should not seek to merely copy the task designs but use them as inspiration for innovative and creative approaches to their own practice, based on sound understanding of theoretical principles from ecological dynamics and applying them using the *Environment Design Principles*.

The structure of the foundation text

This foundation book seeks to provide a sound understanding of the importance of basing practice and training design on the application of a set of powerful theoretical principles. The primary focus is to provide practitioners with a framework to apply the key theoretical ideas of ecological dynamics and nonlinear pedagogy to their practice. To that end, we will introduce the *Environment Design Principles (EDP)*. The book is split into three parts: (i) Theory; (ii) Bridging the gap; and (iii) Practice from theory. Chapters 2 to 4 provide a basic introduction to the theoretical framework of ecological dynamics, which supports a constraints-led methodology. The introductory material is essential for readers unfamiliar with the constraints-led approach and will provide a principled learning design for coaches, specifically focusing on individual-environment mutuality, athletes and sports teams as complex dynamic systems, the nature of interacting constraints and self-organisation tendencies and affordances. Chapters 5 and 6 are the bridging chapters in which we exemplify the tools for practitioners to use to put a CLA into their own practice. The EDP includes a 4-Principle Model, environment and constraints builder tool and a session planner. The framework invites practitioners to systematically design in affordances, constraints, variability and task representativeness to underpin the implementation of a constraints-led methodology. The final part (Chapters 7 to 9) will provide a flavour of the type of content that will be covered in greater depth in the sport specific books in the series. The goal will be to give coaches a 'taste' of what is to come. Chapter 10 (Conclusion) summarises for readers how the main concepts in a constraints-led approach can underpin the quality of practical applications in a variety of sports, encouraging reflection and consideration within the context of each reader's current experience and understanding.

Constraint-led coaching: a new way of thinking

The constraints-led approach (CLA) that originated in the work of Newell (1986) is an integrative model that can also provide applied sport scientists (i.e. in psychological support, strength and conditioning and training), performance analysis with an understanding of how human beings develop or organise movement solutions. While a CLA may have been originally founded on a more dynamical systems model of human movement, recent work has integrated the ideas of ecological psychology and in particular the work of Gibson (1979/1986) and Brunswik (1956). In order to successfully employ a CLA, an understanding of ecological dynamics is essential as these underpinning concepts manifest themselves as guiding principles for the design of CLA practice environments. Applying ideas such as self-organisation under constraints, perception–action coupling and affordances means that practice differs in many ways to traditional methods of teaching and coaching human movement. The CLA is an approach to teaching and coaching based on the fundamental concept of the mutuality of the performer and environment (Gibson, 1979/1986). Through the interaction of the three core categories of constraints – task, environment and individual – a learner will self-organise in attempts to generate effective movement solutions (Renshaw et al., 2010). Thus, the specific goal-focussed behaviours emerge from the co-adaptive interactions to prevailing constraints at a point in time. Consequently, skill acquisition is seen as the development of a functional relationship between the performer and their environment (Araújo & Davids, 2011a; Zelaznik, 2014). The specific focus of practitioners is, therefore, on designing learning activities that allow individuals or groups of individuals (i.e. functioning in teams) to self-organise and co-adapt to changing constraints. Our goal in all the books in this series, and specifically in this foundation book, is to support academics and particularly practitioners who are interested in applying these theories to their practice by adopting a CLA. To that end, we will provide many 'exemplars' from sport and pedagogy settings to help explain the sometimes dense and confronting language that can inhabit the ecological dynamics landscape. In this way, reading a book in the CLA series authored by a coach from a *different* sport can still help practitioners to learn and reflect on their *own work* in the sport of their choice.

General note

Since ecological dynamics, and the concomitant constraints-led methodology is dynamic and continuously developing, it is envisaged that principles of practice will develop at a similar rate encouraging (sometimes subtle) methodological innovations that can be shared. We will seek to integrate nuanced developments into texts, ensuring the maintenance and coherence of a constraints-led methodology, consistent with relevant theoretical principles, empirical research and experiential knowledge.

Part I

A constraints-led approach

The theoretical framework

Part 1

2 A theoretical basis for a constraints-led approach
Background

Coaches, teachers and other practitioners such as applied sport scientists seeking to use the methodologies of a constraints-led approach (CLA) to enhance skill acquisition and learner experiences are faced with a large body of information. The aim of this book series is to provide a nuanced understanding of the ideas and concepts in this body of work. Our aim is to ensure that the main theoretical ideas are accessible to coaches. Some sport practitioners have been using variants of a constraints-led approach in their work, for example to change conditions of practice, without being aware of the theoretical context behind it. While the language used in this theoretical framework can be somewhat technical, there is a lot to be gained by mastering the key ideas because there is a need for theoretical rigour to underpin the development of coaching as a profession. Familiarity and ease with the key theoretical ideas behind the CLA is needed by practitioners since its main methodologies should not be viewed as a *magic bullet* for all learners. Having a solid grasp of the theoretical ideas underpinning constraints-led coaching will help practitioners use pedagogical methodologies appropriately, effectively and efficiently.

So what, 1: we must view practitioners as environment architects

We argue that the role of the practitioner as the environment architect must be given greater emphasis. This perspective is in contrast and proposed as a challenge to the current popular mantra of considering the 'game as the teacher'. While we would agree with the philosophical notions of that mantra, it could lead to practitioners developing an overly passive pedagogical approach. This misinterpretation has led to practitioners being too 'hands-off' at times. An under-appreciation of how nuanced the successful application of a CLA needs to be has led to the provision of rather vague practice environments that lack

(continued)

(continued)

purpose and any form of targeted development. As we note in this first section, sport practitioners need to provide carefully designed environments which make available desired affordances that are functional for athlete performance, adhering to underpinning theories of ecological dynamics.

The CLA is founded on the theory of *ecological dynamics*, which considers athletes and sports teams as complex adaptive systems – a network of highly integrated, interacting sub-components (e.g. parts of the body in an athlete or members of a sports team). In complex adaptive systems, the multitude of parts continually form coordinated patterns (synergies), which are shaped by surrounding informational constraints. Through their interactions, one can identify the coordination states that emerge in a complex system in nature (see Figure 2.1).

A solid understanding of key concepts in ecological dynamics captures the nature of the learner and the learning process for sports practitioners. Viewing learning from this perspective will ensure that coaching practice is informed by theoretical principles rather than by guesswork, the latest fads or fashions, or traditional ways of doing things.

Figure 2.1 The human body is composed of a multitude of interacting components (molecules or neurons, muscles, joints, limbs, bones), which form patterns or synergies to achieve task goals, here identified as a rower training on a Concept 2 rowing machine.

A pause to gather your thoughts: James Gibson (1967) drew attention to a key idea: 'There is nothing so practical as a good theory' (p. 135). To which we would add: without a powerful theoretical framework, sport practitioners might be left at the mercy of outdated practical manuals, Internet forums for untested opinions or simply their own subjective experiences.

The importance of experiential knowledge

The statement from Gibson's (1967) chapter was ahead of its time and it should not be taken to imply that experienced coaches and practitioners need to discard all their own valuable knowledge and insights gained from many days, weeks, months and years of working with athletes of different skill levels. Ideas expressed on Internet forums and blogs can sometimes be helpful and useful for inexperienced practitioners seeking to help athlete development. The *experiential knowledge* of elite practitioners can be useful, as long as it's tested, supported and integrated with *empirical knowledge* of scientists and theoreticians interested in skill acquisition, learning and talent development (Greenwood et al., 2012). Many sport practitioners can be described as *expert without knowing*, whose practice design embraces

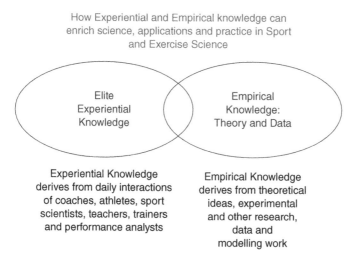

Figure 2.2 How experiential and empirical knowledge can be harnessed by experienced coaches to inform their work with athletes and teams. Inhabiting the space of overlap between knowledge derived by science and knowledge gained from experience can help experienced coaches understand how best to design practice tasks in sport.

a CLA without being able to articulate the technical language behind the methodology that they use in their work.

Figure 2.2 captures how integration of experiential and empirical knowledge, which continually changes as a result of scientific progress and coaching advances, provides a powerful space for solving problems, making decisions, planning, organising and understanding how individual athletes and teams function. Ultimately, these different knowledge sources can support *learning design* during practice in sport.

A pause to gather your thoughts: Consider the question raised by Richard Allen of the ConnectedCoaches blog:

> www.connectedcoaches.org/spaces/10/welcome-and-general/
> blogs/press-release/177/do-we-really-know-how-to-utilise-the-
> constraints-led-approach

Allen refers to the need for coaches to understand the rationale and time and place for manipulating constraints. He calls this the: *how*, *when*, *what* and *why* issues for using constraints manipulations, to which one could add *whom* for an individualised approach. His thoughtful piece implies that it's not simply a case of adding a touch of variability here, or more realism there, in a practice context for learning to magically emerge during a coach's manipulation of a randomly selected constraint or two. Resolving these five issues in practice will provide a substantial basis for using a constraints-led approach in sport.

In the three chapters of Part I, we reiterate the key theoretical ideas in ecological dynamics that underpin the methodologies of the constraints-led approach. We discuss where the ideas originated and their scientific influences so that practitioners may have a better grasp of the framework that underpins the methodologies implied. Having a deep understanding of the key theoretical concepts will help practitioners to use the CLA methodologies to design better learning and development experiences for athletes. To facilitate a deep understanding of the concepts in these initial chapters of the book, readers could continually cross-refer the theoretical concepts to their practical experiences of working with individual athletes and sports teams.

Historical development of a constraints-led approach in sport and physical activity

Where did the concept of *constraints* come from? The word has a special technical meaning in science and has a rich pedigree, having been studied for over a hundred years, particularly in the disciplines of chemistry, physics and evolutionary biology. A fundamental question in science is: how does order emerge in complex physical, chemical and biological systems as they change over time? That is: how do they evolve, adapt, develop, mature, alter, modify, adjust and (re)organise? The answer lies in the surrounding energy patterns in an environment that act as *information* that pressures (i.e. constrains) complex systems to adapt over different timescales (milli-seconds, minutes, weeks, months, years and millennia), resulting in different interactive patterns emerging between system components. Nature abounds with complex systems such as flocks of birds, insects, human societies, sports teams and organisations. Even the multitude of interacting components of the human body has complexity. In complex adaptive systems, spontaneous order can emerge between system components, such as individual fish school-ing together in response to the presence of a predator (see Figure 2.3). Parts of a complex adaptive system can form rich patterns or synergies, which are coordinated states that emerge due to the inherent capacity for parts to self-organise. *Self-organisation* refers to the spontaneous tendencies for adjustment and adaptation of system components to changes in other parts of the system, without the need for executive micro-management of each

Figure 2.3 Nature abounds with complex systems and many biological models to study in understanding how synergies can be continually formed by system components (rich patterns of behaviour) under constraints.

component. Many biological systems, such as a flock of birds, a school of fish, a colony of ants or human movement systems are *open* to continuously exchanging energy and matter with the environment. Complex systems are extremely sensitive to existing environmental conditions and rich patterns can form between system components as energy is exchanged with the surrounding environment.

Complex adaptive systems can influence, and in turn are easily influenced by, the (optical, acoustic and neural) energy flowing in and around them. For example, fish can use on-board sources of energy to swim in any direction in the vast ocean, but instead are constrained by optical information (sight of an approaching predator) to school in rich patterns, swirling to confuse and distract attention.

In sport, individuals are also engaged in the free exchange of matter and energy, moving to provide and perceive information from surrounding energy flows. An invasion game defender engaged in a 1v1 dyad will be attuning to various optical energy flows such as the visual information from the body angle and orientation of the attacker, ball position and the location on the pitch. The defender will also be providing optical energy via the positioning of the leading foot and the distance from the attacker.

Mathematical models have explained how such open, dynamical systems manage to move between different stable states of organisation, depending on the internal and external constraints pressurising (acting on) system stability at any instant. Coaches need to avoid getting bogged down in the common, everyday use of the term *constraints*, which may have negative connotations as a binding or limiting factor on someone. Because of the rich pedigree of the term 'constraints' in science, in this book the term is used in its scientific sense to focus on a feature of the environment which acts as *information to shape or guide the (re)organisation* of a complex adaptive system. Rather than being viewed as negative or positive factors, constraints are best understood in neutral terms. They are best conceived as boundaries that shape the form/structure of a biological system searching for a functional state of organisation (i.e. a state of organisation that can help the system achieve task goals such as moving into space, avoiding other objects or intercepting an object or balancing on a surface). Any change in

---

A pause to gather your thoughts: Constraints are, broadly, information sources that can act over long timescales, such as in evolution, medium timescales such as in growth and development, or in short timescales such as the instantaneous perception of the rabbit or duck (Figure 2.4) in an illusion or spotting the movement differences in a table tennis player's disguised topspin serve.

Figure 2.4 The rabbit and the duck illusion.

the internal or external interacting constraints has the potential to perturb the system and cause instability, thereby promoting a re-organisation of the movement system.

A key point to reflect on is how, at the level of perception and action, constraints shape the behaviours of people during their goal-directed activities.

Interacting constraints in sport and physical activity

In sport, this idea can be applied to the study of athletic performance, as functional coordination patterns in an athlete or sports team emerge under specific constraints, and less useful states of organisation become less stable. In the 1990s, sport scientists became more interested in ideas like this as the powerful theoretical framework behind the constraints-led approach began to emerge. Some were attracted by the potential for an interdisciplinary framework so that sport scientists and practitioners did not have to work in their separate silos. This was a radical idea at that time (and is perhaps still a challenge for some sport scientists and their educators). The importance of interdisciplinarity (or what is now sometimes termed transdisciplinarity) did not have universal approval in the wider sports science community at that time, but it was influential in shaping thinking in some sub-disciplines such as movement behaviour and skill acquisition.

A pause to gather your thoughts: Nowadays, calls for groups of sport scientists to work collaboratively, while adopting an interdisciplinary approach, are embedded in official organisations such as the European College of Sport Science (http://sport-science.org) who noted that: 'scientific excellence in sport science is based on disciplinary competence embedded in the understanding that its essence lies in its multi- and interdisciplinary character'.

A position paper published in the *Journal of Sports Sciences* by Davids et al. (1994) drew attention to key ideas on constraints shaping emergent behaviours in movement systems, calling for a radical overhaul in the way that sport scientists conceptualised coordination and control of actions in sport. This article marked the beginning of a prolonged period of theoretical work that re-conceptualised the nature of athletes' relationships with specific performance environments. The essential thesis of the paper was that athlete performance and behaviours during learning and development needed to be embedded in context to be better understood: That is, the role of the (performance, learning) environment needed to be more carefully considered, to complement the copious efforts devoted to studying individualised traits, and personal features and characteristics of athletes and teams.

So what, 2: the constraints-led approach is not a magic bullet

In its simplest sense, a CLA encourages practitioners to understand and explore how various individual, group and environmental factors impact upon learning and shape the development of human behaviour. This approach requires a deep understanding of context (the sport or activity), human movement (the biomechanics, anatomy, physiology and skill learning of movement), the individual (the psychological and socio-cultural being) and the environment (the learning space we create, and the broader social and political landscape). The development of this holistic understanding allows coaches, teachers, and sports practitioners to appreciate and negotiate these interacting elements in their context, thus developing practitioners who can effectively shape the landscape they provide for their learners. A CLA design is present in all practice environments, from highly structured to unstructured, since interacting constraints (Task, Environment and Person), which the athlete or sports team need to satisfy by continually adapting and (re)organising their behaviours, are ever-present (Newell, 1986).

However, it is most important to emphasise that the CLA is a method that can be employed both successfully and unsuccessfully, and here lies the crucial issue. As highlighted by academics when referring to alternate pedagogies, just because we call it CLA does not necessarily mean it is being used effectively by a sport practitioner (Reid & Harvey, 2014). The CLA is no 'magic bullet'!

This was a radical idea for a theory of movement coordination and control, skill acquisition and sport performance, seeking to establish its scientific credibility at the time. It was specifically argued that current theorising was too narrow and obsessed with a computer or mechanical metaphor for understanding brain and behaviour. This digital emphasis missed the benefits of a natural, biophysical approach in considering the contexts of athlete behaviours. The paper acted as a launch pad for a series of position papers, chapters and books over the next two and half decades, currently framed as the theory of ecological dynamics.

Key theoretical influences in ecological dynamics

Numerous powerful and influential ideas exist in the theoretical framework of ecological dynamics that underpins a constraints-led approach. Key ideas were contributed by: **James J. Gibson** and **Egon Brunswik** on ecological psychology (perception–action coupling, affordances and representative design); **Scott Kelso** on coordination dynamics of brain and behaviour; **Michael Turvey** and colleagues on the functioning of natural physical systems. But the most powerful impact derived from the thinking of **Karl Newell** on how coordination emerged under constraints, operating at different timescales. The original constraints model proposed by Newell (1986) sought to explain development processes in infants and children and did not mention applications to sport performance, skill acquisition, coaching and learning. But within a decade, it had given its name to the methodological model in sports pedagogy that is currently known as the constraints-led approach.

A pause to gather your thoughts: From launchpad to grand unifying framework – the relevance of theory underpinning the constraints framework in sports science is still the subject of intense discussion today. In 2016, Paul Glazier outlined a grand unifying theory (GUT), based on Newell's constraints framework, for understanding sport performance. The purpose of the GUT is to provide a rich, unifying framework to integrate the work of scientists in the many different sub-disciplines that inform sport science.

These influential scientists in the development of a constraints-led approach were somewhat subversive in their thinking, not afraid of going against current conceptual trends in areas like psychology, behavioural neurosciences and movement science. The vision of an interdisciplinary approach to understanding sport performance and athlete development needed a powerful interpretative framework. And it got one, as the relevance of their ideas for understanding coordination in sport performance (Davids et al., 1994), skill acquisition (Handford et al., 1997) and human behaviour more generally, was gradually explored over the next decades.

Key theoretical insights underpinning the constraints-led approach

The ecological psychologist James Gibson (1979/1986) offered innovative insights into the relationship between perception and action, which underpin how constraints shape the behaviours of athletes and sports teams during practice and performance. James Gibson's theoretical work guides practitioners towards appreciating *the importance of context for understanding performance and learning*. This idea derives from the notion that the *person–environment relationship* is the appropriate scale of analysis for understanding human behaviour. In sport, this means that the *athlete–environment relationship* forms the basis of understanding performance and development, rather than the focus on personal qualities only. Scientists and practitioners need to recognise the biases involved in considering athlete performance (i.e. genetic composition, specific movement techniques or patterns of thinking) *separately* from a particular performance environment (e.g. a swimmer's thinking out of the water, a climber's emotions away from a surface such as an icefall or a vertical wall or team games player's performance in static drills away from a game context).

Similarly, there are limitations in considering environmental influences *only* (such as in practice approaches like deliberate practice), without regard for how an athlete's individual *effectivities* (skills, personal characteristics, experience levels and capacities) interact with key environmental properties. According to Gibson (1979/1986) environmental properties provide *affordances* for each individual (opportunities for action). Indeed, certain information sources in a performance environment *invite* actions (Withagen et al., 2012, 2017). With learning, experience and knowledge, athletes can become skilfully attuned to the perceptual variables available in a performance environment to regulate actions. For example, a tennis player who is struggling to 'pick' the direction of his/her opponent's serves at the beginning of a match may begin to notice the patterning of the changes in the hitting action as the match progresses. This information may be found in obvious places such as observing a change in the server's body orientation in volleyball, tennis or badminton, or sometimes from more unexpected sources. A great example of this was recently revealed by the tennis player Andre Agassi who described how he struggled when first playing against

Boris Becker, who beat him the first three times they played. Agassi highlighted that the main reason he could not beat Becker was that he found it hard to pick the direction of his serves. Agassi searched for any sources of information that might give him a clue. Becker kept everything the same whether he served wide or down the middle, with the exception of one unintended and subconscious change that resulted in Becker 'signalling' his intentions. But it took a considerable amount of exploration and searching through tapes of Becker's serves before, eventually, Agassi noticed a key difference: prior to tossing the ball, when Becker served down the middle he put his tongue out in the middle of his mouth, whereas, when he served wide he pushed it to the left side. Agassi could now pick Becker's serve at will and went on to win 9 of their next 11 encounters (www.youtube.com/watch?v=3woPuCIk_d8).

Information regulates actions

According to Gibson (1979/1986), information regulates action and one's actions guide the pick-up of information for further behavioural adaptations. This idea implies that information designed into a practice task (e.g. from: gaps, distances, angles, interactions with equipment and obstacles (Figure 2.5),

Figure 2.5 Interaction of limb segments, muscles, joints and perceptual systems (visual, haptic, proprioceptive) with important equipment during locomotion on road surfaces and pathways in wheelchair racing.

target sizes, surfaces, playing area markings and player numbers in team games) will be used up to regulate an athlete's decisions and actions.

With practice and experience the information in a training context can be coupled to movements in order to modulate, refine and adapt action patterns as they emerge. Does the information need to be *similar* to that which is available in a competitive performance environment? Of course it must, if the information is going to be useful in regulating an athlete's performance behaviours and actions. Does the information need to be *identical* between practice and performance environments? Probably not. Because of the unpredictability of many performance environments, it can be challenging to precisely simulate the exact conditions of a particular performance environment. Practice environments, therefore, can be usefully designed for *simulating* (key aspects of) competitive performance environments. If learning is characterised as the development of effective perception–action couplings, the aim of our practice environments should be to help athletes build these synergies. What determines whether a perception–action coupling is effective? If a coupling between perception and action can help an athlete achieve a performance goal, efficiently, accurately, in a timely manner, and without detriment (e.g. injury), then it is likely to increase an athlete's functionality in performance. This is the crucial point, which is

Figure 2.6 With practice, gymnasts become highly attuned to visual, proprioceptive, haptic and acoustic information in their interactions with equipment (pommel horse), objects (balls and ribbons) and surfaces (floor) in their performance routines.

defined by transfer from practice to the performance environment. Nikolai Bernstein (1967) termed these characteristics of a functional perception–action coupling: *dexterity* in performance, which we discuss in detail later in this section. As a general rule, the more representative a practice environment is, the more likely the perception–action couplings will be able to transfer to a performance environment.

A pause to gather your thoughts: How do you understand practice task designs? Can they be similar or identical to a performance environment? What are the essential aspects of a competitive performance environment that you could seek to design into a practice task? What aspects could you leave out and not impact performance? How far away can you move from the realism of a competitive performance environment without the practice conditions lacking impact on athlete learning?

As will be appreciated, the answers to these questions require some nuanced thinking. Practice simulations may be more and less specific to a performance environment, depending on the nature of the information that a coach wants to design into a practice task. In a constraints-led approach, to ensure that practice tasks specify performance environments, highly specific simulations need to be high in *representative design*. This is a key concept for coaches to understand.

Key concept: what is representative design and why is it important in constraints-led coaching?

The ideas of the ecological psychologist Egon Brunswik (1956) suggest that, for studies of performer–environment interactions (such as those observed in sport performance research), perceptual variables should be sampled from an athlete's typical performance environment, so that they represent the environmental information sources available, and to which behaviour is intended to be generalised. Egon Brunswik (1956) recognised the need to understand behaviour through designing key features of the environment into experiments. He proposed that the 'proper sampling of situations and problems may in the end be more important than proper sampling of subjects' (p. 39).

In science, sampling typically occurs with regards to participants in studies, for example, when seeking correctly categorised samples of elite Paralympic athletes to observe. Representative design emphasises

(continued)

(continued)

the need to ensure that experimental task constraints represent the task constraints of a performance or training (learning) environment that forms the specific focus of study. In the pedagogical practice of coaches, sports scientists and teachers, experimental design equates to the design of practice tasks and training environments. These ideas imply that, as in experiments, the informational constraints of training and practice need to adequately simulate those of a competitive performance environment, so that they allow athletes to perceive information for affordances and couple their actions to key information sources within specific practice settings. To evaluate the representative learning design of particular practice tasks, coaches and teachers should consider the relevance and usefulness (i.e. *functionality*) of the constraints in supporting performers' perception and action in representative performance contexts. In sport, performers need to cope with a range of information sources in a multitude of noisy, messy, dynamic situations, emerging in a performance environment. Only by representing those irregular and uncertain conditions in practice tasks for an athlete can coaches and teachers discover how he/she can achieve a stable, patterned relationship with his/her environment during performance.

These ideas suggest that athletes, coaches, sport scientists and performance analysts need to understand what information sources are used in sport performance to support opportunities for action. These most important perceptual variables need to be designed into practice tasks for learners to use.

The ideas also raise questions over: when, how and why coaches should use grids, cones, ball projection machines, and a whole range of artificial aids as information which constrains actions in learners.

These ideas imply that it is most important to carefully design task instructions (e.g. for directing the athletes' search for perceptual information) and task constraints in practice to help athletes discover and exploit information–action relationships, which underpin successful performance and development (across the whole performance career from novice to expert). During practice, stable couplings will be formed with sources of information that are present in the environment (e.g. climbing only on indoor wall surfaces (Figures 2.7 and 2.8), dribbling around cones, training in a swimming pool, or batting against a ball projection machine in cricket). The question arises whether such practice environments adequately simulate performance. Table 2.1 provides examples of a range of task goals and compares traditional practice methods with alternative RLD-enhanced practice design. A recent real-life example of the limitations of traditional practice to enhance performance was observed in the series of T20 and One Day Internationals (ODIs) between England and India in the English summer of 2018. In the first T20 international, England were soundly beaten mainly due to the efforts of a new Indian wristspin bowler, Kuldeep Yadav. Vadav is a rarity in international cricket as he bowls left arm wristspin. Consequently, many of the England batsmen were unable to 'pick' him (i.e. they could not identify the direction he was spinning the ball) and he picked up three wickets in one over, sending back Morgan (7), Bairstow (0) and Root (0) and creating a collapse from which England never recovered. Kuldeep returned with figures of 5 for 24 and became the first left-arm wrist spinner to pick up 5 wickets in a T20 international. To address this significant challenge to their future success, England resorted to using a special bowling machine, that 'simulates' spin bowling. The views of journalists covering the story, was that this ingenious training aid should make Kuldeep's task much harder in the future with an expectation that the batters would be able to pick up the cues telling them which way the ball was going to spin (see below for a summary).

Jos Buttler [one of the England players] told a Cricket Australia website:

> Kuldeep will have his task cut out with England batsmen now banking on Merlyn – a bowling machine, equipped to simulate any kind of variations, including swing, spin and bowling angles.
>
> One thing we can do is with Merlyn, to replicate the angle. It's a very good machine to get used to that. But it was the first time some guys have faced Kuldeep and it may take one or two games, plus video.
>
> It's about understanding that you shouldn't get too flustered. With spin it can all happen quickly, suddenly you have faced a few balls and aren't off the mark, so it's not allowing that to affect you. You have to get used to the action and once you have faced them a bit more it gets easier. You have a bit more, trust and might pick up a few cues.
>
> Jos Buttler has been assigned to supervise the practice session with Merlyn as he was the only one who seemed to have some clue against Kuldeep.

(www.wahcricket.com/en/news/to-counter-kuldeep-england-adds-merlyn-ahead-of-2nd-t20i-62805)

In contrast to the journalists, anyone who had a background in CLA in cricket might have predicted that Merlin might have had limited impact as there was no opportunity to learn to attune to the specifying information present in the spin bowler's action (Renshaw & Fairweather, 2000). In fact, the impact of using Merlin could have been said to be non-existent, as just two games later, Kuldeep terrorised the England team during the first ODI, with the left-arm spinner finishing with figures of 6–25 from his 10 overs. Obviously, as highlighted by Buttler (the only England player who played him effectively) in the article above, the ideal scenario for England, would be to get some time facing Kuldeep; however, this requires them to stay in! A more effective solution may have been for England to find a high standard left-arm wristpin bowler and face him in simulated game scenarios. For those players who are struggling to 'pick' his action, a constraint could be added in, to direct search to the key information sources within the bowler's action (i.e. the wrist position at ball release). For example, the back of the hand and fingers could be 'painted' with different coloured stripes or he could be asked to bowl with a modified ball (i.e. a two-coloured ball or one with a painted seam) to help the players learn to attune to the key informational cues provided by the bowler. This example highlights that athletes may need to form new couplings during competition, *if* existing perception–action couplings formed in practice environments do not functionally transfer to performance environments. What does this idea imply for the design of training tasks to transfer skill from practice to competitive performance?

Table 2.1 Examples of traditional and alternative RLD-enhanced practice design

Task goal	Traditional method	Alternative RLD-enhanced practice design
Mountain climbing	Indoor climbing wall	Real mountain
Dribbling in team games	Dribbling around cones	Dribbling in a directional practice around an area with other players moving and dribbling
Swimming practice	Swimming circles with other swimmers in a lane	Swimming against others in different lanes. Use of handicapping to experience swimming when leading or trailing
Batting against a spin bowler	Facing the Merlin bowling machine in a net	Facing real spin bowlers in simulated game scenarios
Practising athletic run-ups	Run-throughs (no jump)	Running up to jump in a simulated competition
In play basketball shooting	Unopposed, repetitive, static shooting	Dynamic shooting with the presence of defenders

Figure 2.7 How well does practice on an indoor climbing wall simulate the performance environment mountain climbing? How specific is transfer?

Figure 2.8 What effects on skill could we expect from undertaking an indoor climbing programme? Coordination of actions with respect to the environment.

Ecological dynamics focuses on the importance of *coordination*. This is another important idea promoted by the eminent Russian physiologist Nikolai Bernstein (1967), who placed this concept at the forefront of understanding how humans organise the vast number of system *degrees of freedom* (roughly speaking, motor system component parts such as muscles, joints, limbs and bones). Bernstein's ideas suggest that each individual learner could be conceived as a movement system comprising many interacting *degrees of freedom*. The aim of learning is to ensure that such a complex, multi-component system becomes functionally organised (more efficiently coordinated) as a result of training and practice in sport. This process involves the (re)formation and control of coordinated patterns or synergies between relevant system components, groupings of neurons, muscle complexes and limb segments, during sport performance. The process of synergy formation would be most daunting if it were not for the 'self-organising' tendencies that are intrinsic to complex adaptive systems. In the human body, the self-organising process of synergy formation exploits similar principles that guide flocking tendencies in fish, insects and birds (as we discuss in Chapter 3). Simple rules guide the interactions between individual system components, whether it is a muscle, bone or limb segment. These inherent self-organisation tendencies can be exploited as humans learn to coordinate their actions. Coordination of these motor system degrees of freedom is paramount in achieving specific task goals like jumping into a tucked position in a springboard dive (Figure 2.9) or landing on one leg before springing out into an aerial position in a gymnastic routine.

Figure 2.9 Perception–action coupling in springboard diving.

A springboard diver has to (re)organise motor system degrees of freedom in four different movement sub-phases from the hurdle step, take-off, aerial phase (pictured in Figure 2.9) to water entry. This involves coordination of relevant body parts and use of information from proprioceptive (awareness of body parts in space), haptic (feeling from the soles of feet on the springy take-off board), visual (sighting the end of the board and landmarks in the pool area, as the surface of the pool) and acoustic (sound of the board movement) sources.

It is worth remembering that learners will always attempt to adopt the most functional co-ordination pattern at any moment in time in order to meet their goals and a key role of a coach is to support their search for this solution. Sometimes these goals may be in line with those of a teacher or coach, but at other times, they may be below (or above) the level expected. For example, when first learning to play badminton, the goal of the coach may be to develop an overhead hitting action that enables the player to hit the shuttlecock to the back of the court (i.e. a *clear* shot). For this reason, coaches may demonstrate a 'correct' overhead hitting technique recommended in most coaching manuals and textbooks. The 'clear' requires a significant coordination from several body parts (degrees of freedom), including the legs and trunk as well as the arms and wrist. For the novice, these complex coordination requirements are often beyond their capability and attempts to co-ordinate them all frequently results in complete failure, with 'air shots' that miss the shuttle. Consequently, young players soon modify their own intentions and set their initial goal as simply hitting the shuttlecock and getting it over the net. To do this, they often modify their hitting action using just the forearm to develop a 'tapping' action (see Figure 2.10). This performance solution solves the co-ordination problem by reducing (freezing) the degrees of freedom that need to be organised in action.

Scott Kelso (1995) drew attention to the coordination principles that underpin behaviours of complex systems throughout the whole of nature (from waterfalls to flocks of animals to the brains and behaviours of individual organisms). His ideas on *coordination dynamics* have been influential in understanding organisation in many different systems, whether chemical, physical, neurobiological, or a mix of all features. Kelso (1995) showed that the key principles of coordination dynamics include tendencies for cooperation and competition between system components, often simultaneously, as well

Figure 2.10 Beginner badminton players often freeze up the degrees of freedom to simply 'tap' the shuttlecock back over the net, irrespective of the coach's goal of developing a 'clear shot', where the overhead hitting action enables the player to hit the shuttlecock to the back of the court.

as inherent propensities for pattern formation and self-organisation of system components under constraints. For example, in an invasion game, players on the same team co-operate by creating adaptive interactions as they move with or off the ball. Conversely, the actions of players on opposing teams are coupled together in a competitive way as they co-adapt in attempts to achieve their respective goals. In sport performance, principles of coordination dynamics imply that athletes and sports teams are highly integrated collective systems (e.g. a group of athletes collectively focused on competing in a league). The deeply entwined nature of such systems means that coordination of the vast number of system parts can emerge from continuous changes and interactions between key system variables. Analysis of sports performance through a coordination dynamics perspective seeks to understand how continuous interactions between microscopic elements of a system (e.g. in team games, competition and cooperation of players) result in emergence of macroscopic patterns of behaviour (i.e. global collective patterns of play). In team games this is exemplified by the rich, sophisticated and highly coordinated patterns of movement behaviours in attack or defence shown by performers adhering to simple principles of play such as: advance up the field with the ball, exploit width to increase and exploit space between and behind opponents, and maintain depth to cover space between and behind teammates (Figure 2.11).

So what, 3: it is advantageous for practitioners to adopt a *systems* lens when coaching invasion games

A practitioner will facilitate the creation and application of attacking and defensive systems in a group of players. The role of a defensive system (formation, shape and principles) is to coordinate and organise against any instability caused by the opposition's attacking system. Furthermore, a defensive system may also be designed to cause instability in the opposition's attacking system and facilitate a transition of possession in a more advantageous field position. The team members involved in the system will, via multiple layers (from macro to micro) of perception–action, co-adapt, collaborate and coordinate to achieve their goal-directed behaviours. Practitioners must have the required invasion game knowledge to provide learners with instabilities in practice environments to develop this coordinated organisation.

Michael Turvey (1990) also focused attention on coordination, especially the dynamical interactions between parts of the body that involve two integrated dimensions: (i) the process of organising the functional relations between parts of the body to achieve a task goal (e.g. changing coordinated relationships between relevant parts of the body (e.g. between the hip, knee and ankle to transition from walking to running); and (ii), (re)organising parts of the body with respect to environmental objects, surfaces,

Figure 2.11 Perceiving a gap between defenders and coordinating action
   accordingly in team games.

implements, other people, spaces, gaps, terrains and so on (Figure 2.12). His
research shows how perception is needed to regulate our actions, and we
act to perceive, because information about the world and the body facilitates emergence of adaptive, functional behaviours in performers to satisfy
changing task and environmental constraints.

A pause to gather your thoughts: Turvey's focus on coordination emphasised the importance of understanding how processes of perception and action are highly integrated. Turvey pointed out the challenge for scientists and practitioners in designing experiments and practice tasks, respectively, by pointing out that (1977, p. 211):

> it is curious that theories of perception are rarely, if ever, constructed with reference to action. And, while theories of perception abound, theories of action are conspicuous by their absence. But . . . perception and action are interwoven, and we are likely to lose perspective if we attend to one and neglect the other; . . . After all, there would be no point in perceiving if one could not act, and one could hardly act if one could not perceive.

So what, 4: practitioners should encourage self-organisation

This understanding often leads practitioners to direct a learner's attention within the environment, informing them of where and what to perceive (in information terms). For example, it is important for practitioners to help learners with 'where to look', but not restrict their search strategies by being overly prescriptive and telling them 'what to see'. This approach is useful with different sources of perceptual information such as proprioceptive, haptic and acoustic information. The environments that practitioners design will allow learners to self-organise and attune to the relevant energy flows.

> Experts . . . encounter an environment overflowing with opportunities, and they single out from among the available opportunities just those that are relevant to their interests, preferences, and needs in the specific situation.
>
> (Rietveld & Kiverstein, 2014, p. 341)

It is the role of the practitioner to facilitate and encourage this process through the application of a CLA.

In ecological dynamics, the term skill acquisition refers to the process of acquiring an increasingly functional (more efficiently coordinated and effective) relationship with a particular performance environment. The large number of motor system degrees of freedom available for an athlete

Figure 2.12 Turvey (1990) emphasised the importance of the perception–action
relationship in coordinating parts of the body with respect to
movements of other people and objects in a dynamic environment.

can be considered a 'blessing' since it is a rich and wonderful resource to
be exploited when adapting actions to dynamic, information-rich environments. For this reason, *skill adaptation* would be a better term to describe
the process of an athlete becoming more skilful in a sport. This subtle change
in emphasis would avoid the idea that 'acquiring skill' involves the personal
acquisition of an 'entity' (i.e. skilled behaviour) or a status (i.e. high skill
level) by an individual. Skill adaptation is essentially defined as enhancing
one's functionality in a performance environment, which can continually
be improved (Araújo & Davids, 2011a). Captured this way, learning is a
process by which an athlete's behaviour becomes better adapted to a specific performance environment. By increasing or reducing the involvement
of motor system degrees of freedom, the athlete can temporarily assemble
stable, flexible and functional actions (a process known as '*soft assembly*').
This idea signifies that these synergies emerge under constraints and are
not permanently hardwired into the skeletomuscular system to help them
achieve their intended task goals.

    Skill adaptation implies that performance goals can still be achieved,
as athletes learn to vary their actions according to the information that
emerges in unpredictable performance contexts. Adaptation provides a
functional relationship between *stability* (i.e. persistent behaviours) and
flexibility (i.e. variable behaviours) during performance. Highly skilled

> Skill acquisition is better framed as skill adaptability as it involves forming more functional relationships with a performance environment.

performance is characterised by stable and reproducible movement patterns, which are consistent over time, resistant to perturbations. Bernstein (1967) showed, with his work on hammering a nail, how skilled individuals do not achieve consistency through repeating an *identical* movement pattern time after time. Their actions are reproducible only to the extent that a *similar* movement pattern may be re-organised under the same task and environmental constraints. Skilled athletes exhibit stable patterns of behaviour when needed but can vary actions (subtly or not) depending on the demands of dynamic performance conditions. That is the basis of dexterity according to Bernstein's (1967) proposal, which we mentioned earlier in this section as the basis of the effectiveness of a perception–action coupling strengthened in practice. Athletes' actions become more stable and economical with experience and practice. Yet stability and flexibility are not opposing characteristics of skilled performance. Flexibility should not be construed as a loss of stability, but as a sign of skill adaptation, as motor system degrees of freedom are continually re-organised to achieve specific performance goals, solve problems and satisfy the demands of competition. This is a key idea for coaches as learning designers. It implies that variability needs to be designed very carefully and thoughtfully into practice tasks to enhance athlete skill adaptation. By designing learning environments in which each learner is continuously challenged to adapt to varying task constraints, coaches and teachers can support learning, psychological preparation and conditioning for sport performance. Here we need to go back to the questions of: *why, when, how, what* and *whom*, during manipulations of task constraints. The answers to these questions are developed with an understanding of the end in mind, namely *optimal grip*.

The enhancement of expertise in different sports domains through implementation of a constraints-led methodology is characterised by an individual having an *optimal grip* over the field of affordances (Bruineberg & Rietveld, 2014). Skilled performance is also predicated on context-sensitive actions. This notion stretches our understanding of what the learner is searching for as they self-organise during practice – that is, they are searching for an optimal grip. Similar to a player trying to (re)organise their biomechanical degrees of freedom, a player is also searching for optimal grip on the field of affordances. Skilled *intentionality* is what an individual exhibits when acting skilfully in a familiar situation or as characterised by Bruineberg and Rietveld (2014) – the tendency toward an optimal grip on a field of affordances.

A pause to gather your thoughts: These ideas on flexibility, stability and skill adaptation seem to be modern insights promoted by ecological dynamics, but they are remarkably aligned with ideas of Bernstein (originally proposed in the Russian language in the first half of the last century, but translated into English in 1967, p. 228): Dexterity is: *'the ability to find a motor solution for any external situation, that is, to adequately solve any emerging motor problem correctly* (i.e. adequately and accurately), *quickly* (with respect to both decision making and achieving a correct result), *rationally* (i.e. expediently and economically), *and resourcefully* (i.e. quick-wittedly and initiatively)' (italics in the original).

The concept of degeneracy: a platform for skill adaptation

Practice task design could incorporate variability into learning contexts to encourage athletes and teams to seek different solutions to the same performance problem, as well as requiring athletes to explore a variety of related task problems to find the same performance solution. In neurobiology, this is known as exploring system *degeneracy*. **Degeneracy** is another technical term that needs to be understood in its strict scientific sense. In a complex adaptive system, degeneracy has been usefully defined by Edelman and Gally (2001) as '. . . the ability of elements that are structurally different to perform the same function or yield the same output' (p. 13763). In movement behaviour, system degeneracy supports the great flexibility, adaptability and robustness needed for an athlete's functionality during performance. Functionality of athletic performance in skilled athletes is exemplified by coordinative structures assembled to achieve a particular task goal in different ways (Figure 2.13). Degeneracy in the movement system supports the interchange of different sub-structures in achieving a task goal. In an individual athlete, degeneracy involves the (re)organisation of different muscle groups, joint combinations and limb segments (motor system degrees of freedom) to coordinate actions to achieve the same task goals. For example, in relatively stable performance environments, like archery or shooting, performers can exploit system degeneracy to constrain their actions, depending on subtle changes in influential variables like wind direction or strength, ambient temperatures or the layout of the competition venue. In more dynamic performance environments, degeneracy can be harnessed for re-assembly of the same motor system degrees of freedom to achieve different performance outcomes. In a sports team, this process refers to the rotation of roles between players and the interchange of players in different sub-phases and tactical patterns during performance. The actions of individual performers can be constrained by co-positioning and re-alignment of move-ments of teammates and opponents, as game events emerge, field surfaces change due to weather conditions, or properties of the ball or projectile alter with humidity and presence of moisture, or due to sudden changes in opposition strategies and tactics.

So what, 5: examples from sport

In the Atlanta Olympics in 1996, Australian hockey coach, Rick Charlesworth developed an approach that enabled his team to play at a much higher tempo than other teams. Charlesworth worked out that the humidity in Atlanta would result in teams playing slower than normal. To counter this, he developed a policy of rotating his players to keep them fresh. To do this he needed players to be able to play more than one position, ensuring that his team were highly adaptable. The tac-tics worked, with Australia winning the gold medal. System degeneracy provides each athlete with opportunities to exploit the deeply inter-twined relationship between their cognitions (i.e. specific patterns of thinking, ideas, intentions, beliefs and desires), perceptions and actions. It underpins the stability and flexibility of coordination patterns used by each athlete in competitive performance. The degenerate architecture of athlete movement systems provides a platform for creativity, innova-tion and adaptability during learning and performance. The take-home message here is that learners need to be provided with practice task con-straints that allow them to explore dexterity in their interactions with the performance environment. Exploration and, ultimately, exploitation of inherent *degeneracy* is a major goal for learners during continuous interactions with key features of a practice environment, which coaches need to emphasise in their learning designs.

From a practical perspective, these ideas imply that coaches need to ensure that athletes have plenty of opportunities for continually adapt-ing their actions (re-organising their motor system degrees of freedom) to achieve same/different task goals under varying performance conditions. This is what athletes and sports teams need to excel at during their constant repetitions during training and practice. The continuous re-organisation of system components during learning to achieve the same or different task goals is aligned with Bernstein's (1967) proposal for practice to consist of **'repetition without repetition'**. His ideas suggest that repetitive practice should not merely consist of repeating the same movement pattern time and again, (i.e. repetition *after* repetition), for example, when trying to repro-duce a 'classic' forehand drive in tennis or in replicating the 'ideal' textbook

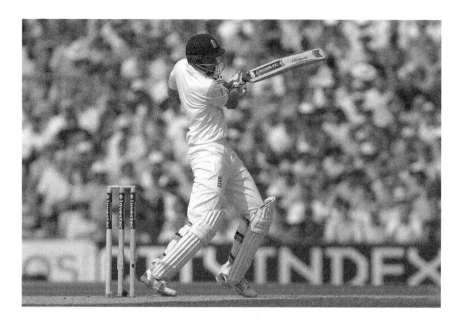

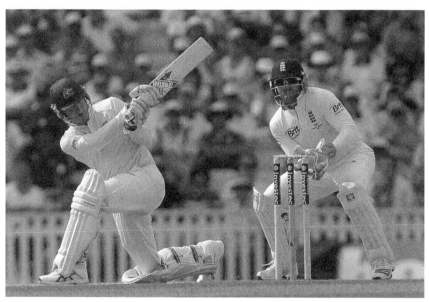

Figure 2.13 Humans can show wonderful adaptability and flexibility by exploiting
inherent motor system degeneracy. Athletes can use different
coordination patterns and parts of the body to achieve the same task
goal, here striking a ball with a bat.

stance in archery. Rather, due to changing performance conditions, learners should be challenged to repeat the process of solving the same performance problems under varied practice task constraints.

This conceptualisation of how to design practice tasks and programmes fundamentally opposes the traditional view of creating conditions for constant *reproduction* of an ideal movement so that specific neural pathways in the nervous system are strengthened, or traces in an internal movement representation are refined. Traditional pedagogical practices also tend to: (i) meticulously structure detailed learning tasks into isolated sub-phases, (ii) elaborate tasks into progression-drills, often in static and unopposed contexts, and (iii), are typically decomposed into manageable sub-movements for repetitions. This traditional approach is exemplified by the assumptions behind the popularity of spring board divers practising separated movement sub-components in isolation away from the pool in a 'dry-land' facility using foam pits, or batters in cricket and baseball rehearsing aspects of their 'technique' against a ball projection machine. The ideology behind this traditional way of practising separate task components is based on the assumption that separately practised sub-components can be successfully re-integrated into the whole diving or batting action.

There is no question that using the traditional approach requires a coach to be highly organised. However, this approach often involves methods of *task decomposition*, which can lead to the decoupling of information and movement, for example, when a learner practises dribbling around static objects like cones, instead of passive (and then active) defenders in small-sided and conditioned games. This atomised approach helps guide learners vertically through progression-drills. These strategies, based on whole-part task training, guided by verbal instructions/feedback, have the unfounded assumption that performing components of a task, in isolation, will unproblematically

Figure 2.14 Practising in the dry-land area of a diving programme. Here, athletes practise tasks that are decomposed to emphasise the hurdle step and preparation for take-off phase separately from the aerial and landing phases (for safety reasons).

lead to successful performance of the entire task when parts are re-integrated. This traditional pedagogical approach follows a logical progression from known to unknown, simple to complex and easy to difficult, as task components are 'mastered' in isolation (Figure 2.14).

The assumption of additive part–whole learning is a long-held idea, whose proponents argue that skills where the parts 'remain the same' are best suited to the task decomposition approach as it allows 'stable schemas for movement sub-components' to be developed and then put together. For example, tennis serving is proposed as one such task where there is 'clear evidence that practicing the subtasks in isolation can transfer to the total task'

Figure 2.15 Volleyball serve on the 'readying' phase unopposed.

(Seymour, 1954 cited by Schmidt & Young, 1986, p. 23). The underlying assumption behind application of this idea to pedagogical practice is that the sub-tasks are essentially independent activities and there is little difference in performing them apart or as a coordinated whole action, since tennis serving is considered to be made up of two separate motor programmes that run sequentially (i.e. the ball-toss backswing as the first programme and the second programme that produces the hit) (Schmidt & Young, 1986).

However, there is limited evidence in support of this theoretical explanation with empirical research questioning the efficacy of additive approaches in skill acquisition. A number of studies have shown that breaking actions down to improve modules or sub-phases leads to limited transfer when moving back to performance of the whole task. However, in tasks such as tennis or volleyball serving, coaching manuals have tended to follow the motor programme model of part–whole learning emphasising that a consistent ball toss is crucial to the success of the serve. This approach has resulted in coaching practice that focusses on developing a stereotyped ball toss in isolation from the 'hitting action'. It is common practice for coaches to place a small hoop or chalk a circle on the court surface and require players to practise throwing the ball up to land inside the small area. Only when consistency is achieved in this task sub-component do coaches then 'add in' the hitting sub-phase of the serving action. However, expert tennis and volleyball players do not actually achieve invariant positioning in the vertical, forward-back and side-to-side toss of the ball. Handford (2006) examined the serves of senior international players performing the volleyball serve and found that the only invariant feature of their serving action was the vertical component of the toss, with the forward-back and side-to-side dimension showing high levels of adaptive variability. It would appear that the server only aimed to create temporal stability in terms of the time from the peak height (zenith) the ball reached and the time required for the forward swing of the hand to contact the ball (Figure 2.15). Interestingly, in a study to compare the ball toss characteristics in part and whole tasks, the variability of the peak height of ball toss when undertaking part practice separately and the mean value for peak height *was much greater* than in the whole condition. It would appear that decomposing the task led to movement patterns that were dysfunctional for performance. The key to learning to serve is to link perception to action together to effectively support performance.

Breaking up a movement into separate components for isolated practice therefore fails to recognise how separate parts of a multi-articular action are co-dependent on each other for successful performance. Such complex coordination patterns are difficult to decompose because of the information that establishes 'coherent integration' between parts during performance. Practice strategies should typically avoid undermining the deep relationship between parts of a coordinated action through task decomposition. Rather, parts of a synergy needed to achieve a performance goal need to be kept together during practice. Scaling or simplification of an action for an athlete, rather than decomposition during practice, would be an ideal way to help athletes seek functional performance solutions, while allowing conditions to vary. Many elite sports coaches and practitioners intuitively understand this key idea.

A pause to gather your thoughts: Pep Guardiola, one of the best football coaches in the world, noted that: 'Football is the most difficult game in the world because it is open, and every situation is completely different, and you have to make decisions minute-by-minute.' (Pep Guardiola, 2016: www.theguardian.com/football/2016/oct/07/pep-guardiola-exclusive-interview-johan-cruyff-unique).

The dynamic nature of the ecological constraints of competitive performance dictates that practice needs to involve 'repetition without repetition' in many different sports, regardless of whether their ecological constraints are more or less static or dynamic. In the context of sport practice, 'repetition without repetition' refers to the need for learning designs to place athletes in dynamically varying contexts where they have to repeat problem solving and find a way to achieve a specific task goal or realise a particular intention. This principle of practice involving 'repetition without repetition' applies to many different sports like archery, gymnastics, climbing, springboard diving and shooting, not just team games like basketball and the many codes of football. The emergence of behaviours under manipulated constraints is a key idea that needs to underpin the design of practice tasks that require athletes to solve performance problems with their actions. In adapting to changing interactions of constraints, athletes can learn to exploit adaptive variability to maintain the functionality of their performance behaviours.

3 Interacting constraints and self-organisation tendencies

In Chapter 2 we argued that a most significant challenge in sport concerns the continuous re-organisation of movement system degrees of freedom during performance to produce functional solutions. Human beings can adapt actions continuously by exploiting inherent movement system *self-organisation tendencies*, which are available to all biological organisms, such as bird, fish and insects.

Choreography in the sky: A wonderful example of self-organisation tendencies in open systems exists in a *murmuration* of starlings, small birds that gather in vast numbers to spontaneously swoop and swirl at high speed at dusk, forming rich patterns of coordinated behaviours on the wing. This breath-taking video clip shows how the movement of each bird influences the co-adaptive movement of immediately adjacent birds and from these local interactions comes global pattern formation. The movements are not pre-planned and orchestrated but emergent under the constraint of interacting locally with nearby birds:

(A Murmuration of Starlings https://vimeo.com/31158841).

Ecological Dynamics argues that spontaneous self-organising tendencies also exist in the movement systems of athletes (e.g. when running on a track [more quickly or slowly, when facing a head wind or in slippery conditions]). Tendencies for self-organisation under constraints can be exploited in many dynamic performance contexts. (For example, when running on a variety of surfaces (stable and unstable) such as rocky trails, race tracks (when wet or dry), sand dunes or mud. They are also important in the interpersonal interactions of competing and cooperating team games players performing on different surfaces, indoors and outdoors, in different venues and against different opposition playing styles and in varied game formats.

In sport, self-organising coordination tendencies emerge within and between individuals as they engage with the task and performance environment. These coordination tendencies can support *intra–individual–environment* or *inter–individual–environment* interactions. They result in the formation of localised synergies between body parts in an individual athlete (a coordination pattern to achieve a specific performance goal) or between team members (a pattern of interactions in an attacking phase of play or in a defensive unit). Inter-individual co-ordination tendencies also emerge between opponents, for example, when an attacker tries to run past a defender. System interactions spontaneously emerge when previously uncorrelated components (neurons, muscles, joints in an individual performer or teammates and opponents in a sports team) form groupings or synergies that are interrelated and entrained under ecological constraints of competitive performance environments.

Complex adaptive systems like athletes and sports teams display these hallmark properties of *synergy formation under constraints* and *sensitivity to surrounding information*. In different sport performance contexts, a key strategy is to identify the nature of the information that constrains self-organisation tendencies over different timescales. Synergies in movement systems and sports teams are *temporarily assembled* to achieve specific performance goals. Because synergies can be rapidly put together and dissolved quickly, athletes and sports teams can enjoy both stability and flexibility of action. They are flexible, stable and exquisitely context-dependent, meaning that synergies are rapidly adaptable to changing circumstances. The functionality of a synergy (i.e. its usefulness and relevance for supporting performance) evolves over time through experience, practice and learning: more useful and relevant synergies are strengthened, and less useful ones are de-stabilised over time because of their growing irrelevance. In an invasion game context, a defender will self-organise and manipulate the body and foot position in a 1 v 1 situation to channel an attacker away from goal and apply appropriate pressure on the ball. This type of body orientation towards the opponent and the ball is a temporarily assembled synergy. If the attacker changes his/her attacking angle, speed or direction, the previous synergy will become irrelevant and a new synergy will be required. In this respect, skill acquisition (i.e. skill adaptability) is an evolutionary process, rather than a revolutionary one.

A pause to gather your thoughts: While self-organising tendencies can spontaneously emerge in athletes and sports teams, they can be exploited by applying specific task constraints during practice to shape the formation of stable, yet adaptable synergies. This is why it is always a good idea to consider that *self-organisation tendencies emerge under constraints*, so that these processes can be exploited in learning designs for specific performance behaviours.

Newell's model of interacting constraints

In Newell's (1986) model, interacting constraints have been defined as boundaries or features that shape the form of a complex adaptive system searching for functional states of organisation. Performance functionality implies being able to make sense of a particular performance context and then to carry out intended tasks and activities during behaviour that is goal-directed. Constraints act to reduce the number of configurations available to a complex, dynamical system at any instance. They help to structure the number of possible system configurations for an individual. It should be pointed out that system configurations are based on the current action capabilities of an individual or team at any one time. This might mean that the emergent co-ordination patterns may not fit the optimal movement solutions often reported as 'classical techniques' in coaching books. However, these emergent movement patterns may be the best fit in terms of what the individual's intentions are at a specific point in time. For this reason, coaches of young performers should not consider their performance in the same way as they may view adult performance levels. Children are not mini-adults, but rather are at varying stages of development and maturation which constrains their behaviours.

There are many classes of constraints that can shape the behaviours of a complex dynamical system and it has been well documented that Newell (1986) considered individual (termed 'organismic'), task and environmental constraints to be the most influential (see Figure 3.1 for some examples). Organismic constraints refer to the personal characteristics of each individual, such as genes, height, weight, muscle-fat ratio, cognitions and patterns of thinking, amount of previous experience and learning, motivation, emotions, feelings and desires. They need to be considered carefully by coaches since such personal constraints vary between and within each individual over different timescales. They can be influenced by factors operating over timescales of learning (hours, days, weeks) and maturation, ageing and development (months and years). Environmental constraints are more global, and can consist of physical variables in nature, such as ambient light, temperature, or altitude, or social features such as historical, cultural and societal values, beliefs and customs. Task constraints are more specific to performance contexts than environmental constraint and include task goals, specific rules associated with an activity, use of activity-related implements or tools and particular surfaces or objects involved in performance (Davids et al., 2008).

What can we learn from evolutionary science?

Constraints are specific to performance niches and operate at many different levels of the system or the environment and at various timescales. This is what makes them challenging to use in practice task design (the 'what', 'how', 'when', 'whom' and 'why' questions raised earlier). Organisms are also shaped by system pressures over longer timescales in an evolutionary process, where

Examples of interacting constraints on the emergent behaviours in sport		
PERFORMER	TASK	ENVIRONMENT
Cognitive skills, emotional capacities, mental attributes, goals, motivations, intentions	Specific rules, markings, boundaries, surfaces	Family support and networks
Physical constraints including strength, speed, flexibility, height weight, and acoustic and visual system function	Instructional constraints including coaching methods, types of feedback provided, exposure to discovery learning etc.	Cultural expectations and attitudes. Social construction of age, gender, race etc.
Genes	Use of video, images, stimulations and models for practice	Peer group pressure, media images, commercialisation of sport and physical activity
Specific activities undertaken during practice time	Design and scaling of practice equipment	Access to high quality facilities for training
Amount of learning and previous experience	Design of practice tasks: Task simplification vs Task decomposition	Access to high quality learning opportunities and teaching
Develop status of various subsystems including those for locomotion, postural control, reaching and grasping etc.	Artificial aids and devices	Physical constraints such as gravity, altitude, ambient lighting and temperature.

Figure 3.1 Examples of interacting constraints.

personal constraints interact with environmental constraints. At the level of a species, they are allied to selection as part of the evolutionary process that guides biological organisms toward functionally appropriate behaviours in a particular niche or habitat. This idea from evolutionary science can be applied to understanding sport performance behaviours. When a talented young games player moves up to the next performance level, in team games for example, the time and space available to perform skills is generally decreased and the young learner must adapt his or her actions to successfully survive and then thrive in this new performance niche. The relationship between the organism and the environment defines a 'form of life' for that species. This concept can be applied to the context of sport and exercise by defining different units within a team as a separate 'species' all with their own forms of life. Defenders, midfielders, forwards and goalkeepers, for example, could all be viewed as different species. A squad of club players could be defined as different to a squad for international athletes, with a different niche in the world and, therefore, different forms of life. A niche is a set of multi-dimensional affordances for a particular individual (Chemero, 2003; Heft, 2003). We will discuss this concept in more detail in the following chapter.

At the performance-relevant timescale of perception and action (microseconds or fractions of a minute), constraints operate to select emergent patterns of behaviour in a continuous '*adaptation + feedback*' loop. In sport performance, functional patterns of behaviour can be explored and refined over time by athletes as they emerge under interacting constraints. Coaches could understand how to interact personal constraints of individual learners (e.g. training status, level of experience, skill needs) with specific task constraints, such as performance space, time, properties of objects and implements used, and task goals of practice. Environmental constraints could also be integrated into the most efficient of practice designs by harnessing weather conditions, travelling to train at altitude and by simulating social and cultural constraints of competitive performance environments. Cultural environments are important factors that should be carefully considered by practitioners. Culture is an important component of the 'form of life' of coaches in sports (as introduced previously and discussed in depth in later chapters) and is shaped by the history of practice and by practitioners in the moment, in terms of what they say to learners and performers in addition to how they lay out the physical environment. Cultural constraints are, therefore, shaped as much by the philosophy of the practitioner, which sits within the culture of an individual sport, organisation or school ethos. In Chapter 4 we examine the important effects of social and cultural constraints in more detail.

In order to ensure a close simulation of competition conditions, the interaction of categories of constraints during practice should be continuously framed by cognitions and intentionality of athletes: that is, performance during practice should always be framed by striving for specific goals, objectives and aims of an athlete or sports team. Framed intentionality forms the basis of the 'adaptation + feedback' loop that guides an athlete's motivation and performance awareness during practice.

Through manipulation of key interacting constraints, more functional (relevant and useful) patterns of behaviour gradually become more stable over time, and less functional states of system organisation are destroyed (due to their instability). Sport practitioners should allow athletes to gain experience in exploring a variety of task designs, learning how to find performance solutions that are most functional and then continuously refine them through exploiting feedback loops. The notion of 'adaptation + feedback' underpins Bernstein's (1967) conceptualisation of practice as 'repetition without repetition'.

How cognition, perception and action support goal-directed behaviours

In performance and practice, the process of establishing a stable perception–action coupling (the basis of skilled performance) is deeply integrated with knowledge predicated on specific intentions and cognitions. An athlete maintains *contact* with a dynamic performance environment by continuously using his/her cognitive activity and perceptual information to guide interactions.

For example, a performer may decide to: reach and grasp an object moving in space, or avoid an individual running to make a tackle, or accelerate through a gap between two opponents, or simply to stand still. An athlete's *intentionality* expresses their cognitive activity through anticipation, memories, attention and decision-making. Intentions, perception and action are completely intertwined, functioning in an integrated way, and none of these processes can function in isolation of each other. One cannot act without perceiving and one cannot successfully perceive information from the environment without acting. The implication for practice is that this continuous coupling of perceiving and acting needs to be continually framed by an athlete's intentions.

It is worth noting that Kelso (1995) viewed *intentions* as a most important source of constraint: a specific informational constraint that could be used to stabilise or destabilise existing system organisation, depending on needs, wishes, desires of an individual. In sport, intentionality is very much related to skilled performance and the capacity to select amongst available affordances. Skilled intentionality (Kiverstein & Rietveld, 2015) is defined as 'the individual's selective openness and responsiveness to a rich landscape of affordances' (p. 701). This is the fundamental essence of decision-making in sport, which coaches can harness and develop in training designs: adaptive behaviours can emerge continuously from the confluence of constraints framed by intentions embedded within agreed and negotiated task goals.

These ideas suggest that it is important to design opportunities for action that allow athletes to continuously seek perceptual information from a learning context to couple with their intended actions. In the next sections of this chapter, we will discuss some examples of how skill may be enhanced by allowing localised action solutions to emerge as internal and external system conditions change. This 'adaptations + feedback loop' harnessed by athletes, using representative practice task designs, can lead to a tight coupling of perception and action sub-systems during performance.

To summarise so far, Ecological Dynamics is an integrated framework with four features of significance for understanding sport performance and how it can enhanced in practice: (i) the individual–environment relationship is the fundamental level of analysis for scientists and practitioners wishing to understand performance and learning in sport; (ii) behaviours emerge from self-organisation tendencies in multiple subsystems; (iii) interacting constraints shape these emergent behaviours; and (iv), designing opportunities for action or affordances into landscapes for learning can guide individuals to use actions to explore perceptual information available.

Manipulation of constraints in individual sports

An important personal constraint in sport is the experience and expertise that an individual brings to the performance context. Ecological Dynamics highlights how the nature of perception–action couplings is not the same for beginners and experts, since the expert is more capable of exploiting information about environmental and task-related constraints in order to continuously reorganise the multiple degrees of freedom of the body. The greater adaptability of experts to a variety of interacting constraints emphasises the functional role of movement variability in supporting sport performance. Movement system degeneracy allows a skilled performer to explore different motor solutions, facilitating the discovery of functional patterns of coordination. By harnessing system degeneracy, with practice, a learner can structurally adapt his/her motor organisation without compromising function in order to satisfy task constraints (gaining feedback that strengthens the possibility of the action re-emerging in similar situations in the future). In complex performance environments, skilled athletes are able to perform several types of movement and/or to switch between synergetic modes of coordination in order to achieve the same functional performance outcomes. This capacity for flexible variability in exploiting motor system degrees of freedom for achieving task goals was demonstrated by Hristovski et al. (2006), who investigated how boxers adapted their strike patterns when they were asked to punch a heavy bag from various distances, without any precise verbal instructions. The task was simply to hit the heavy bag as hard as possible with any boxing action. At further distances from the boxing bag, a 'jab' action with a straight arm tended to emerge, whereas at close distances 'uppercuts' or 'hooks' patterns appeared. Intermediate distances from the boxing bag represented a meta-stable performance region (i.e. where a range of useful behavioural solutions could emerge). In this region, varied and creative range of movement patterns occur such as 'uppercuts', 'hooks' and 'jabs' (Hristovski et al., 2006). These observations suggested that the boxing striking patterns transitioned according to the perception of a 'strikeability' affordance (i.e. the perception of distance information to a target invited certain actions). This type of affordance-based regulation of action has also been reported in other individual sports like rock climbing. Boschker et al. (2002) previously analysed the perceived structural features of climbing walls and climbing opportunities (defined 'climbing' affordances by Boschker and co-workers). The results showed that unlike the beginners, expert rock climbers were able to utilise more information and perceive the functional properties of the climbing wall, showing greater exploitation of climbing affordances. Rock climbing affordances include hold *reach-ability*, *grasp-ability* and *climb-ability*. Note how all these affordances emphasise opportunities for climbers to interact with important surface features. An important consideration is the interaction between an individual's intentions and how they perceive the environment. For example, a beginner level climber who is focused on not falling off the rock will attune to different affordances (e.g. closer holds that help them maintain a forward facing orientation to the rock) than an experienced climber who is looking to move up the rock face fast (e.g. potential holds that require body orientation changing to be 'side-on' to the rock). Interestingly, skilled climbers were only as good as the novices in perceiving the *structural features* of the climbing wall, such as colour and or hue of the surface. This type of knowledge is based on perceptual processes that support a verbal description about the environment. Gibson (1966) called this 'knowledge about' the environment. According to Gibson's (1977) ideas, knowledge about the environment can be learned indirectly via exposure to images, pictures, video analysis or other sources of symbolic information, which facilitates the provision and sharing of explicit information between athletes and coaches. One example of this type of knowledge occurs when a coach communicates specific information (principles of performance) to athletes, in a learning environment (coaching session), or even in a team meeting or briefing session preceding performance. This may involve instructing an athlete when and how to act in a specific performance situation. Through verbalised/pictorial/graphic information, a platform of shared knowledge can be designed that may be collectively internalised among athletes and support staff, thus allowing shared understanding and coordination of activity (Figure 3.2). For example, a coach may show video clips of opponents to direct her players' attention to specific features of an opponent's movements or specific patterns of play.

In contrast, Gibson (1977) proposed that *information for action* is predicated on 'knowledge of' the environment, which supports the perception and utilisation of affordances. This type of information can be designed into practice environments full of invitations for the emergence of different

Figure 3.2 Verbal instructions have value in guiding the search of athletes for functional task solutions during practice. Verbal guidance should be composed of 'knowledge of' the environment to invite athletes to seek and utilise affordances in a performance landscape.

performance behaviours. This emphasis in learning design provides opportunities for *interactions* allowing athletes to seek, discover and exploit affordances to support performance in specific sport contexts.

This idea was exemplified in an intervention study investigating affordances designed into traditional training practices in elite springboard diving. Barris and colleagues (2014) studied preparation for take-off in an elite sample of Olympic-level springboard divers when diving into a pool and under the different task constraints of training in a dry-land facility comprising a foam pit. Elite divers tend to routinely practise in separate training environments (dry-land and pool), affording differences in final performance outcomes. The watery surface of a pool afforded penetration with the hands of the divers, whereas the harder texture of foam pits in the dry-land facility afforded landing feet first. Divers seek to practise the same preparation phase, take-off and initial aerial rotation in both practice environments, although there is little empirical evidence to suggest that the tasks completed in the dry-land training environment are representative of those performed in the pool environment. The concept of *conditioned coupling* in Ecological Dynamics signifies that performance of different movement components would remain dependent on each other, and slight variations in task constraints could lead to different emergent coordination patterns (Davids et al., 2013). In line with these theoretical predictions, it was expected that emergent self-organisation tendencies under the affordances of the two distinct task constraints would lead to differences in preparation. Barris et al. (2014) observed similar *global topological* characteristics in all participants who used the same joint coordination patterns during dive take-offs completed in the dry-land and aquatic environments. However, as a group, participants showed statistically significant differences in performance at key events (second approach step, hurdle step, hurdle jump height and board angles during the hurdle and at landing) during the preparation phase of dive take-offs completed in dry-land and aquatic training environments. For example, participants showed significantly less board angle depression at landing (from the hurdle jump) during take-offs completed in the dry-land area ($M = 14.27$, $SE = 0.24$), than those completed in the pool ($M = 15.99$, $SE = 0.26$). It is possible that the different affordances of the distinct learning environments may have led these subtle differences in performance behaviours to emerge. The findings highlight the sensitivity of learners to the design of learning tasks since such subtle differences in actions emerged under the different task constraints.

Manipulation of constraints in team sports

Manipulation of task constraints in team sports has mainly focused on understanding how coordination emerges from interactions between players within and between teams, under the constraints of competitive performance. Passos, Araújo and Davids (2016) summarised work on the continuous interactions that emerged at different scales of analysis (between *dyads* – in 1 v 1 situations – and between and within *sub-groups* – attacking and defending units of players).

Dyads

A considerable amount of research has sought to identify coordination patterns in attacker–defender dyads in team sports over the past two decades. Dyadic systems are formed by *1 vs 1* interactions during performance and are considered the basic unit of analysis for studying interpersonal coordination tendencies in team sports (Passos et al., 2013). Dyadic system relations in competitive matches reveal the pattern forming dynamics that are the essential unit of analysis for understanding how the microscopic degrees of freedom (competing team sports players) co-adapt their actions during performance.

Research suggests that successful performance in team sports demands that athletes learn how to interact with teammates and opponents to achieve their goal. The continuous interactions that emerge as athletes co-adapt to each other's behaviours are constrained by locally created information from the actions of each individual involved in a dyadic system (Passos, Araújo, & Davids, 2016). This information emerges from interactions with a range of different task constraints, including field locations, markings and boundaries, and rules, which act as boundary constraints on the relative co-adaptations of players. A significant source of information that constrains performance behaviours is the relative co-positioning of interacting players during performance as they compete to find/restrict space and time and achieve performance goals. Research has shown how actions of performers are continuously modified due to the presence and location of significant others onfield. For example, Orth et al. (2014) investigated the characteristics of competing attacker–defender dyads in football, investigating how performers modulated their running velocity to kick a stationary ball, under the constraint of defensive pressure. Approach velocity and ball speed/accuracy data were recorded from eight youth players, as they ran to cross a ball to a teammate in an attacking position. Defensive pressure was manipulated in three counterbalanced conditions: without defenders present, with a defender positioned far away, and with a defender positioned near the player crossing the ball. Findings showed that players altered their actions under changing task constraints without any instructions from the experimenters. For example, ball speed during the cross was significantly reduced as defensive pressure increased by locating the defender closer to the starting position of the attacker. In footfalls during the final approach to the ball, running velocity was dependent on both presence and initial distance from a defender as a key task constraint. Despite these changes to movement organisation, passing accuracy was maintained under changing defensive pressure by the skilled footballers. Overall, the results showed how the regulation of kicking behaviours is specific to the design of a performance context. Some features of movement organisation emerge under varying task constraints, for example as the presence of a defender is manipulated during performance.

Another study investigating dyadic system behaviours in soccer by Headrick et al. (2012) showed how field location for performance constrained the regulation of action by players. They sought to determine whether spatiotemporal relations between players and the ball in 1 vs 1 dyadic systems were constrained by their distance to a goal area. They observed each participant performing as an attacker (dribbling the ball) and defender. The modification of the distance of the dyadic system to the attacking goal area shaped players' behaviours and intentionality. A key variable 'defender's-distance-to-the ball' appeared to be a critical collective variable. The percentage of trials in which the player in possession of the ball dribbled past the defender revealed higher success rates in positions closer to the goal. The implication for coaches here is that even the smallest modifications to the details in the design of practice tasks can shape the interactive co-adaptations between players in 1 vs 1 dyads.

Sub-phases of play during practice

Dyadic systems represent the basic scale of interaction within many team (invasion and field) games; research also suggests that more complex sub-phases of play are important for understanding the patterns of coordination emerging when players form larger synergies during performance. The implication of these studies is that small-sided and conditioned games (SSCGs) provide an opportunity to practise performance in a sub-scaled version of the whole, formal game. Different SSCG formats can effectively condense and specify constraints of competitive performance contexts and help to potentiate the emergence of specific technical and collective tactical behaviours (Ometto et al., 2018), as well as to provide opportunities to experience physical, physiological and technical demands of competition in a contextualised simulation. An important benefit of SSCGs is that they provide coaches with opportunities to manipulate key task constraints, such as player numbers involved, as well as space and time, which aid the development of tactical intentionality in players during different sub-phases of play. The development of tactical performance behaviours depends on task design since a well-designed SSCG simulates key aspects of the competitive performance environment. This enables players to reproduce the behaviours needed in the type of dynamic competitive environment where there are opportunities for players to experience the 'repetition without repetition' that Bernstein (1967) envisaged was the cornerstone of relevant practice.

For example, 2 vs 2 in basketball can provide a useful context for learning many different skills and basic tactical patterns when attacking, transitioning and defending in the team sport. Similarly, 7 vs 7 in rugby union can be relevant for gaining increments in physical conditioning, tactical understanding and skill acquisition. Indeed, SSCGs are also useful for experiencing the structural and functional patterns that emerge in full-sided versions of a game. An important consideration for practitioners is to consider the representativeness of the SSCG in terms of the full-sided version of the game. Failure to do so would only lead to the transfer of generic skills rather than specific skills (ideas, perceptions and actions), which would be less useful in the full-sided game.

Coaches often refer to the 'centre of gravity' of a team during play. An operational definition of this concept is a team's centre (also known as centroid, or geometrical centre). This measure has been used in various ways to evaluate intra- and inter-team coordination during sub-phases of play in team sports. Team centres can represent, in a single variable, the relative positioning of both teams in forward-backward and side-to-side movement displacements of sub-systems (e.g. 3 vs 3 in basketball or 4 vs 4 in football). Principles of play in team sports suggest that the team in possession of the ball should seek to create space by stretching and expanding the team centre in play (increasing distances between players), while a defending team should restrict space by contracting and reducing distances between players. Such collective behaviours have been captured by specific measures of team coordination in performance analysis that quantify the overall spatial dispersion of players in play. The *stretch index* (or *radius*), the *team spread* and the *effective playing space* (or *surface area*) are measures that record such spatial distributions. Also, it is important for a successful team to outnumber the opposition (creating numerical *overloads*) during different performance phases (attack and defence) in specific locations adjacent to the ball, expressed through inter-team coordination variables. These measures capture the existence of possible differences in players' interactive behaviours at specific locations on field (e.g. wings and midfield sectors). Research in sub-phases of football has shown how the centroids of competing teams approach and move away from each other's defensive lines in a systematically interrelated (ebbing and flowing) manner, particularly just before loss of stability. The emergence of such characteristics was stimulated to a prominent degree by the distance values between an attacking and defensive line of players, which suggests that the design of SSCGs needs to consider the effects of playing area dimensions on tactical behaviours that emerge during practice. Likewise, emergent playing patterns in SSCGs (4 vs 4), measured by centroid positions and surface area measures of competing teams, displayed synchronous tendencies to move in the same directions during a competitive game. Findings revealed a stronger association between forward-backward and lateral oscillations of centroids. There is still a need for more research to understand whether the dynamics of some collective variables (e.g. team centroid and surface area) that emerge during performance in SSCGs, with a reduced number of players (e.g. 3 vs 3, 4 vs 4, 7 vs 7), correspond to patterns observed in full-sided games.

The micro-structure of practice

What should coaches/teachers have in mind when they use a constraints-led approach to design effective practice tasks and learning activities, undertaken daily, weekly and monthly, in preparation for the physical, psychological and emotional demands of competitive performance? The *micro-structure* of practice, day in-day out, involves pedagogical activities that include tasks designed, constraints manipulated, intentions harnessed, emotions experienced and adaptive interactions required of athletes continuously during learning. Adopting an individualised approach, based on the needs of specific athletes, coaches can vary the nature and intensity of these sport performance aspects. Well-considered manipulations of constraints should create individualised problems and challenges for learners, which simulate key aspect(s) of a performance environment (whether physical, cognitive, emotional, social or a mixture of these features).

Facilitating athlete dexterity in the micro-structure of practice

As previously mentioned, *all* coaching methodologies involve constraints manipulations of some sort. However, traditional pedagogies tend to focus on a narrow range of constraints being manipulated in practice, especially early in learning, to ensure that athletes can repeat actions and rehearse movement patterns in drills. Sometimes, to make matters worse, drills designed in the micro-structure of practice are performed at low-intensity levels in static conditions, with minimal information being present.

All athletes, whether beginners, advanced learners or experts, can benefit from using their cognitions, perceptions and actions in an integrated way to solve problems that they may encounter during competitive performance. Solving performance problems and meeting challenges with actions enhances 'dexterity' in individuals. That is why practice task constraints should be designed to encourage exploration of relevant performance solutions needed in competitive environments. Exploratory activity is an integral part of human development and babies (for example) spend a lot of time in their infancy exploring the environment to learn about affordances of objects and surfaces and other people (Gibson, 1988). Continuous exploratory interactions with the environment, termed 'experiments on the world' by Gibson (1988, p. 7) are typical in human development and lead to skills that can be harnessed in later athletic development when people start to specialise in competitive sport.

Through continuous interactions with equipment, space, other individuals and events, during sport training and practice, athletes can be supported by coaches in exploring the range of affordances available in a perceptual-motor landscape of possible performance solutions (Davids et al., 2016). Practice needs to help athletes develop individualised and contextually functional motor solutions, rather than to rehearse and reproduce a collective 'default technique' or optimal movement 'template', towards which all athletes should aspire (Brisson & Alain, 1996; Chow et al., 2016).

Figure 3.3 Drills in practice are over-used, emphasising repetition and rehearsal of specific movement patterns in static performance conditions, rather than the search for functional action solutions.

Designing opportunities to display dexterity during practice in tennis and rugby union

This Bernsteinian perspective emphasises that a fundamental aim of practice is not to 'optimise' performance of specific movement pattern through repetition and rehearsal. Rather, dexterity implies athletes enhancing their skill in co-adapting to the conditions of a performance environment. To achieve this aim, practice micro-structure should continuously seek to present each learner with a wide range of tasks and conditions that they need to explore. This type of design would enhance the dexterity of an athlete by helping him/her to become more adaptive, innovative and flexible to cope with variations in task and environmental constraints. For example, in the sport of rugby union, a challenging decision is when to kick the ball upfield to create attacking opportunities and when to run at a defence with ball in hand. Designing an 'affordance field' in practice, athletes can be encouraged to co-adapt their decisions and actions to what an opposition's defensive pattern invites. Athletes can be required to adapt their actions throughout an unfolding practice game, employing a kicking game against the opposition depending on what their defensive strategy offers them. Essentially, coaching in these games involves asking players to consider 'where is the space?' and 'what are the best ways to get the ball in the hands of a team mate/player in that space?' – something we address in Chapter 5 when we present the *Environment Design Principles* for coaches. If the defence leaves the full back behind the pack (forwards) alone, with the defending wingers also playing high up the pitch, performers may be encouraged to notice the spaces around the full back that invite them to kick the ball more frequently into these areas. If the wingers hang back, then it means that there is more likely to be space around the outside of the defensive back line, inviting a potential overload situation if the ball can be moved wide quickly enough. Therefore, kicking more or less frequently, when attacking, will emerge, depending on what the defensive formation affords for the attacking team. Coaches could change affordances in the micro-structure of practice, making sure that, every day, training and practice abound with problem solving scenarios, just as implied in Bernstein's (1967) ideas on developing dexterity.

Being able to perceive and use affordances, as opportunities for action, is a major feature of each individual's capacity to co-adapt to task and environmental constraints which coaches can facilitate in the designs they use for practice. This idea has been exemplified in the work of Anna Fitzpatrick and colleagues in tennis, a sport known to be initially challenging to become proficient at, due to the coordination demands of manipulating a racket to intercept a ball travelling at high speeds, the movements required to cover the relevant court areas and tactical behaviours needed when playing against opponents with different characteristics (tall, fast, left-handed, power-serving, to highlight a few), in singles and doubles tournaments.

Fitzpatrick et al. (2017) considered that, when designing practice tasks in tennis, scoring format, court dimensions, net height and ball characteristics are key task constraints. Manipulating these constraints in practice enables inexperienced participants to perform, without the need to contend with the challenging constraints of the full version of the game. However, it is important that the modified practice environments help to simplify performance constraints, allowing learners to maintain and enhance perception–action couplings required during performance in the full version of the sport. For example, a tennis ball with reduced compression will bounce lower on court, facilitating young players' forehand and backhand performance, by allowing them to adopt a swing height that is scaled to their current body dimensions. This re-scaling in practice is useful for the long-term development of their groundstroke skills, compared to the racket swing height needed to strike a regulation tennis ball that bounces higher on court. Evidence suggests that the constraints favoured within mini versions of tennis influence emergent behaviours of players during practice. To exemplify, tennis balls with low compression levels positively influence children's forehand groundstroke performance. Reducing ball compression from 100% (i.e. regulation tennis balls) to 75% has been reported to increase the amount of net-play and elicit a better bounce height for young children learning to hit the ball with groundstrokes, re-scaled to their dimensions. Fitzpatrick and colleagues advocated that the use of modified tennis balls, providing a longer flight phase and lower bounce height due to lower compression, should enable participants to maintain control of rallies for longer, in turn facilitating the development of a wider range of strokes. They summarised previous research into the effects of manipulating court dimensions and net height on emergent behaviours of skilled young players on court. Evidence from research showed that, although average rally length did not differ between conditions, smaller court dimensions elicited fewer winners, and a reduced net height elicited a greater number of winners. Fitzpatrick and co-workers (2017) concluded, therefore, that manipulating key task constraints, such as reducing court dimensions and net height, created a relevant environment for young children learning to play tennis. An interesting video on YouTube shows how modifying court sizes, racquets and ball types can lead to junior games that are highly representative of the adult games. Essentially, the video clearly demonstrates how the junior game can be adapted to 'look and feel' like the 'real' game (www.youtube. com/watch?v=3IbzcttoDuY&feature=youtu.be).

Harnessing self-organisation tendencies when coaching

The examples from rugby union and tennis suggest how coaches can use task constraint manipulation as a basis for designing practice tasks that can exploit the tendencies for self-organisation that exist in humans (Figure 3.4).

It is clear that the role of verbal instructions is minimised, and direct teaching or coaching is only used when needed by a coach. In other words, verbal instructions and direction is simply another tool in the 'methodology' of a coach. However, direct verbal instruction tends to be over-used in pedagogical practice and is often 'over-advocated' in coaching manuals and courses. It tends to be viewed as a 'default' methodology that many coaches view as absolutely essential to their practice. There is evidence that constraints manipulation is effective in helping learners to acquire skills and maintain a high level of engagement and motivation in sport and physical education contexts, as exemplified by the work of Brendan Moy and colleagues (Moy et al., 2014, 2015). In their work, they demonstrated that allowing novice hurdlers to choose the level of difficulty when presented with a row of hurdles of different heights and distance apart enhanced perceptions of competence, autonomy and relatedness. If early coaching experiences are as much about hooking children into sport, these findings are debatably just as important, if not more so than the actual skill learning that did take place.

Coaches are ultimately responsible for planning and structuring practice programmes by selecting from a variety of particular task constraints to attune each performer's attention to relevant information sources in performance settings. Their role is to manage intended self-organisation processes of individual and team tactical behaviours in achieving a specific objective to be accomplished in different phases. The main challenge of

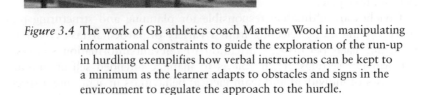

Figure 3.4 The work of GB athletics coach Matthew Wood in manipulating informational constraints to guide the exploration of the run-up in hurdling exemplifies how verbal instructions can be kept to a minimum as the learner adapts to obstacles and signs in the environment to regulate the approach to the hurdle.

performance coaches is to develop the excellence of an individual athlete or team in practice by harnessing self-organisation tendencies of individual and team behaviours, concomitant with the application of particular intentions or tactical principles. During practice, self-organisation tendencies can be *managed*, *driven* and *guided* by a team coach in each phase of a competition, delimited primarily by the definition of performance intentions and tactical principles, agreed in the athlete-coach relationship. By manipulating specific key task constraints during coaching sessions, coaches may provide important information sources or shared affordances (agreed upon opportunities for action relevant collective sports and games) that support a specific communication system between athletes (or between athlete and coach), allowing self-organisation tendencies to be exploited. During preparation for competitive team games, for example, players learn to couple actions to form an interpersonal synergy (e.g. functional grouping of two or more performers in attack or defence). The couplings emerge from self-organisation or adjustments between teammates and are strengthened during practice, underpinned by the collective perception of shared affordances. The concept of shared affordances is key in team sports and requires an intimate knowledge of one's own affordances or action possibilities, those of team mates and those of opponents. It is clear that creating effective inter-personal couplings is very demanding and only the best team seems to possess this knowledge. Players need to be given time to create synergies where every player intuitively knows how a team mate is going to act at any one time.

4   A landscape of affordances

According to James Gibson (1979/1986), an affordance should not be viewed as an entity or object, but rather as a functional relationship formed between an individual and a particular (aspect of a) performance environment. Gibson argued that: 'The affordances of the environment are what it offers the animal, what it provides or furnishes, either for good or for ill' (p. 127). This idea signifies that, in sport, athletes need to be adaptive to pick up information to utilise affordances available in different performance environments. There is some selectivity involved since not all affordances are functional for all performers (providing 'good' outcomes) and some affordances can lead to problems such as negative outcomes, injuries or poor health ('ill'). This connotation of affordances has some important implications for the way that coaches can design practice activities in sport, especially with reference to the individual needs of a performer.

Competitive sport exemplifies environments that provide a manifold of action possibilities, which are uniquely *relative* to an individual, requiring specific experience, development, skill and intentions to utilise. Due to differences in these qualities, the opportunities for action in a performance environment that can be utilised by a professional athlete will differ from those used by a recreational athlete to support behaviours. Gibson argued that 'Affordances do not cause behaviour, but constrain or control it' (1982, p. 411). These ideas suggest that affordances can be viewed as important constraints that need to be understood, relative to each athlete, in the design of practice micro-structure. The implication is that task constraints in part of an affordance landscape (Rietveld & Kiverstein, 2014), can be designed by coaches and teachers to *invite* specific actions from different athletes, depending on their intentions and other personal constraints, such as physical and psychological characteristics.

Gibson (1979/1986) was very clear on the social significance of affordances for humans interacting with other humans. The richest affordances are provided by the behaviours of other people that can be perceived and utilised through interpersonal interactions. As Gibson (1979/1986, p. 135) pointed out: 'Behavior affords behavior'. These affordances have the highest level of 'behavioral complexity' (Gibson, 1979/1986, p. 137), implying the need for immense skill in perception of information from others, and anticipation of their actions, which can help in regulating one's own intended performance outcomes. Practice task designs need to enhance athlete skills in perceiving the shared affordances of and for other individuals during performance. This particular point has significant implications for designing practice tasks in sports that require continuous interpersonal interactions in team games or against opponents in duel-based competition (e.g. racquet sports, fencing or combat sports) (Chow et al., 2016; Davids et al., 2016; Maloney et al., 2018; Silva et al., 2013).

How climbers use affordances to regulate their performance behaviours

An affordance-based mode of performance regulation helps a performer to perceive information variables that are most relevant (i.e. be perceptually attuned to constraints of the performance environment) and be able to use the information to guide their actions, based on experience, skill level and key body dimensions, such as limb sizes. For example, with practice, an ice climber can become better attuned to information from the properties of a frozen waterfall, gaining knowledge of what is being offered by gaps, holes and structures in the surface (Figure 4.1). For this reason, climbing actions have been categorised as *exploratory* (actions seeking information about surface or hold properties) or *performatory* (actions that move an individual from point A to point B on a surface). Perception of information from an ice fall can be supported by actions such as hitting or tapping the ice to check whether these properties afford hooking with an ice tool or kicking with a crampon in order to support body weight. Highly skilled ice climbers display greater perceptual attunement to visual, acoustic and haptic sources of information, which allow climbers to detect 'use-ability' (affordances) of existing holes in an icefall. When ice is relatively soft or ventilated, climbers can anchor their ice tools in one swing, whereas when ice is dense and thick, climbers often need to repeatedly swing the tool to acquire a deep and stable anchorage. Expert climbers can typically detect variations in icefall thickness (for example, by listening to the sound of the ice tool contacting the ice or by feeling the vibrations from the tool-ice contact). This acoustic and haptic information helps them to reduce frequency of actions needed to acquire strong and stable anchorages, saving energy. In contrast, beginners are mainly concerned with safety, avoid falling. They are mainly attuned to visual characteristics of an icefall, focusing on size and depth of holes and steps, since big, deep holes are synonymous with more secure and stable anchorage. They tend to mechanically repeat the same actions to create a deep hole for anchorage, wasting energy. Finally, low levels of accuracy may lead to more exploratory movements and errors (in which a movement does not completely fit with environmental properties), leading to falls.

Figure 4.1 An ice climber uses an ice hook and crampons to traverse the surface of a frozen waterfall. Information from the vibrations of the ice hook on the surface (haptic), sound of the tool engaging the holes in the ice (acoustic) and the colour of the ice (vision) is used by the climber to regulate their actions during the ascent.

A pause to gather your thoughts: Climbing has been added to the list of sports for the 2020 Olympic Games. Performance occurs in many environments, including: indoors (wall climbing) and outdoors, on surfaces of varying heights, short (e.g. up to a maximum of 7–8 m height in 'bouldering') or long ascents (e.g. from one pitch to multi-pitches averaging 20–30 m each), at low or high altitudes, on rocky, snowy, icy, or mixed surfaces and terrains, with or without tools for support (e.g. ice tools, crampons and ropes), in a sport format (with bolts) or traditional (without bolts), and with more or less engagement with other climbers (e.g. solo, top-rope, or on-sight). During performance a climber needs to perceive information on ice or rock properties, assess risk of avalanches, anticipate weather events using forecasts, maintaining a possible fall-back option or an escape route. This degree of environmental uncertainty, coupled with related psycho-emotional and physiological demands involve on-going adaptations that distinguish expert and non-expert climbers. *Adaptability* is vital for skilled performance because of the continuous co-adaptations of individual climbers to the dynamically changing, interacting constraints, which are perceived and acted upon.

Using guided discovery in the micro-structure of practice: how a well-designed affordance landscape can help learners to become more adaptable

Coaches, sport scientists and performance analysts can collaborate to design practice tasks that help athletes learn to adapt their actions to key objects, features, terrains, conditions, characteristics and significant others in a performance environment, to achieve their intended task goals. This design aspect of their work targets the micro-structure of practice: that is, the daily, weekly and monthly planned activities that can gradually help athletes function more effectively in a specific performance context. The micro-structure of practice theoretically contains a rich landscape of affordances, opportunities for perception, action and cognitions that athletes can experience during practice. In Figure 4.2, this landscape of inviting opportunities is presented in a continuum in which the affordances available can be picked up and used by an athlete, or not, depending on needs, experience and skill level. The affordance landscape continuum ranges from being quite narrow and limited at one end (constrained by prescription and instructional constraints of a coach or teacher) and rich and varied at the other end, as captured in unstructured practice and play environments or when tasks are designed to facilitate exploratory behaviours and discovery learning. In some parts of the practice landscape there are fewer affordances, with narrower task constraints and fewer opportunities for action and in other parts of the continuum, there are situations with less narrow task constraints, which invite a more diverse range of behaviours. The challenge for coaches is to understand *where* on the practice landscape continuum each learner needs to be, *when* he or she needs to be there, *why* he or she is best placed at that location on the continuum, and *what* practice activities need to be designed for an individual learner at that point of the landscape.

There are pedagogical methodologies associated with different parts of the practice landscape in Figure 4.2. Coaches can locate a practice task design at different parts of this affordance continuum, designing a practice micro-structure accordingly, depending on the needs of each athlete at a particular time. The default approach in sport pedagogy tends to involve spending inordinate amounts of time in low intensity practice contexts, *simply rehearsing repetitive movements,* within a narrow field of affordances (Figure 4.3). That is: spending more time at one end of the continuum, coaches rely on specific methodologies like verbal instructions and rehearsal of a movement pattern or team play.

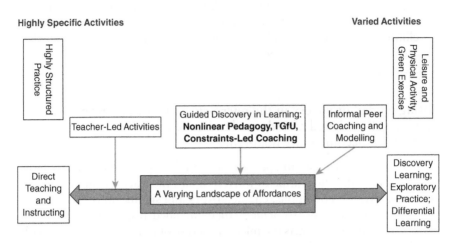

Figure 4.2 A continuum of practice task designs.

The landscape of affordances forms the continuum of practice task designs from highly structured to less structured environments. Learners can be guided to seek and utilise the affordances at different parts of the landscape, depending on their current needs. Generally, less time should be spent at the highly structured end of the practice design continuum, because the

Figure 4.3 The role of the coach in repetition and rehearsal.

methods used at this end tend to be too prescriptive and directing. Coaches tend to move to the highly structured part of the continuum and design tasks that learners explore under narrow task constraints.

Coaches will agree that repetition and rehearsal is needed during practice. However, coaches need to decide on the amount of time spent using these methodologies and the value gained from them. There are also question marks over the intensity levels of practice. Do the practice task constraints adequately simulate the performance conditions? Are the practice tasks representative of performance environments? What is the purpose of the rehearsal and repetition and how much time is needed in these practice task designs?

This more traditional approach to practice may not be needed all the time by different athletes. It depends on the needs of the specific learner. Rather, athlete dexterity can be enhanced through providing opportunities for learners to *discover* and *exploit* functional action solutions in a varied field of affordances, with a diverse range of opportunities to act from which an athlete can select a solution to improve performance effectiveness. This key idea was shown in the study of a boxing heavy bag's 'strikeability affordances' that we discussed earlier. A simple practice design feature of manipulating the distance that an athlete is positioned from a heavy bag to punch, can change the actions that emerge during practice without the need for precise verbal instructions from a coach. In this way an athlete can enhance his or her dexterity by exploring different ways of striking a bag without being under explicit directions.

What role do verbal instructions have in the design of an affordance landscape in practice?

Information made available through task constraints manipulation (e.g. changing the distance and orientation between hand hold grips on an indoor climbing wall) can support and direct the exploratory activities and search behaviours of learners during practice (e.g. two-finger and three-finger grips that are horizontally and vertically oriented on the wall). A constraints-led approach suggests that a simple re-orientation of climbing grips on a wall can help climbers learn to re-organise available motor system degrees of freedom (in the hands and feet) to achieve the intention of ascending a route safely and rapidly (Orth et al., 2016).

Verbal instructions as augmented feedback: what is their role in learning design?

What do these findings imply for the role of verbal instructions, or other forms of explicit communication, which are dominant, perhaps over-used, traditional methodologies in sport pedagogy and teaching? What happens when learners do not display exploratory tendencies during practice after extensive manipulations by a coach? Clearly, there will be some learners who will challenge the innovative creativity of coaches and teachers in appropriately manipulating task constraints to elicit emergent performance behaviours. The affordance landscape described in Figure 4.2 suggests that there is a role for verbal information to guide the search activities of learners, which stimulate them to develop functional patterns of behaviour. Verbal information, used sparsely and selectively, could impact on motivation and effort of learners during practice, by helping to locate them in the relevant 'field' to direct search in an affordance landscape. Verbal instructions (more explicit, directive communications) can manage and direct the self-organisation tendencies of individual and teams, during practice sessions, because they can direct an athlete's attention to specifically-available affordances. A major problem is the *over-use* of verbal instructions and explicit communications, such as a nod of the head, and pointing with hand signals, *as direct informational constraints* that take away the autonomy of athletes in making their own decisions during performance. Rather than explicit direction, verbal or otherwise, the aim should be to use such communication methods as informational constraints that guide athletes towards the information available for their own decision-making, thinking and movement organisation. More specifically: verbal instructions and explicit communication forms used in a command style to direct a learner's actions or those of a performer in competition can prevent individuals from finding their own performance solutions.

So how can verbal instructions and explicit communications best be employed in pedagogical practice? They can provide a pedagogical tool that can serve to direct athletes to affordances that they can seek, discover and exploit in a landscape of opportunities available. Verbal instructions can be used for shaping emergent decision-making processes and exploiting self-organising tendencies in athletes, and coaches must carefully utilise these augmented informational constraints (Figure 4.4).

This is because poorly applied, verbal instructions can interfere with athlete decision-making, autonomy and movement organisation, increasing attentional loads of performers and disrupting their ability to satisfy task constraints with their own actions. Instructions and feedback can be best implemented when athletes cannot acquire information for task performance through their own exploratory behaviours. This may happen, for example, in team games at an early phase of tactical development, when players may not be familiar with principles of play. Coaches could provide verbal information to direct performers to attend to specific information variables that could support their decision-making and individual/ collective behaviours, aligned with particular performance objectives. As quickly as possible, when functional patterns of team organisation have been established and understood by athletes, coaches could reduce the amount of verbal information given to performers, freeing them up to seek and utilise affordances available in a performance environment.

Figure 4.4 Infrequent use of verbal instructions can help athletes search, discover
and exploit affordances in a performance landscape.

The take-home message here is that verbal instructions and direct guidance
should be used sparingly, carefully and thoughtfully by coaches, especially
ensuring that athletes have plenty of opportunities to search an affordance
landscape for themselves.

Creating a form of life in practice: harnessing socio-cultural (environmental) constraints on skill adaptability and expertise

In this chapter we have suggested how designing an affordance landscape
can help individual athletes search fields that are particularly relevant to
competitive performance needs. In elite performance and athlete development programmes this aim could underpin a *form of life*. As discussed
earlier, a form of life refers to the nature of the socio-cultural practices that
have been historically embedded in societies, communities, organizations,
educational establishments and in elite and sub-elite sports programmes
throughout the world. In everyday language, perhaps this is what coaches
and sports administrators mean when they talk about the 'DNA' of a team
or sports organization. The term *form of life* has a deep philosophical herit-
age, being coined by the philosopher Ludwig Wittgenstein to describe the
behaviours, skills, capacities, attitudes, values, beliefs, practices and customs

that shape the culture, philosophy and climate of societies, institutions and organizations (Rietveld & Kiverstein, 2014). In short: a form of life shapes the way we do the things we do.

Rothwell, Davids and Stone (2018) proposed how *forms of life* are founded upon specific socio-cultural, economic and historical constraints that have shaped the development of performance in a particular sport or physical activity. Examples of 'forms of life' in sport include basketball in North America, winter (snow and ice) sports in Northern Europe, endurance running in East Africa, sprinting in Jamaica, soccer in Brazil, cricket in South Asia, swimming in Australia, rugby league in northern England and rugby union in New Zealand. Often, a form of life can shape a unique way of performing that dominates a sport in a specific society or community, for good or bad. Even in our globalised world, a form of life can dominate the way that young athletes are taught basic skills through coach education, customary ways of performing, leading to role modelling and continued prominence of performance models that are valued by local populations because they are aligned with societal values, customs and world views. Given these ideas, a form of life can provide a unique advantage to a group of athletes or hinder their progress as measured globally.

Analysis of the socio-cultural and historical constraints in particular societies can explain the forms of life that have emerged to underpin highly identifiable performance styles and athlete development in specific parts of the world, why specific ways of performing are valued in these communities and exploited to establish dominance in elite sport. To exemplify, Uehara and colleagues (2016) discussed the form of life that emerged from the historical immigration patterns and socio-cultural constraints of Brazilian society that shaped the way that local inhabitants participated in soccer, dominating world rankings for decades. Socio-economic developments shaped the impoverished conditions of interwoven sections of Brazil's immigrants in the early part of the last century leading to affordances for social expression of power through a soccer style captured by 'ginga' (playing with flair) and 'malandragem' (the art of trickery and cunning in play). Other cultural and historically specific activities like samba (a type of rhythmic dancing popular in Brazil) and capoeira (a local type of martial art) also influenced the way that Brazilian soccer players express themselves in movements. The qualitative analysis of the knowledge of elite soccer players and coaches in Brazil by Uehara et al. (2018) revealed that a successful outcome of a competitive match is not enough. The way that victory is achieved is also important in the form of life underpinning specific performance expression in soccer. The form of life in Brazilian football values playing with flamboyance, flair, trickery, passion, confidence and style. This form of life is predicated on a rich mix of individuality of expression with the ball and embracing the needs of team work. It is based on highly specific customary, habitual modes of performing, competing, training and practising, modelled through different cohorts of performers, throughout the decades, in both structured programmes and unstructured contexts. In sports, a form of life in specific sports is predicated on deep socio-cultural and historical roots, making it infeasible for one society in another part of the globe to simply imitate an identifiable performance style associated with another (highly successful) society.

In sport, the *macro-scale* form of life (emerging over decades of sport experience) in a society, community or geographical location, shapes the design of practice programmes at a *micro-scale*. The micro-structure of practice refers to the day-to-day activities that form practice and athlete development programs. In these societies there is a firm attachment of coaches, underpinned by beliefs, attitudes, values in coach education programs (whether official or unofficial) to the design of specific types of *affordance landscapes* in athlete development programmes (Davids et al. 2017; Rothwell et al., 2017; Uehara et al., 2018). It is important to understand how a form of life can help sport practitioners harness local socio-cultural practices, shaping opportunities for action in developing athletes in initial, unstructured interactions in informal play environments. These initial experiences can influence how athletes use affordances during skill acquisition and expertise development in formal practice programmes and in informal activities. Understanding more about this issue can help sport practitioners to identify and exploit key socio-cultural constraints in designing an affordance landscape in specific sports (Davids & Araújo, 2010; Uehara et al., 2016).

When designing a learning environment, coaches need to consider each individual athlete's current available experience, abilities and capacities, captured in their *intrinsic dynamics* (dispositional tendencies). In constraints-led coaching, affordances are not merely action opportunities offered by an environment but depend on the particular needs and capacities available to each athlete in a particular ecological niche such as a sports training program. This conceptualization of affordances is based on the mutual athlete–environment relationship, which underpins a particular *form of life* in a society or an organisation. In a dynamic context, with sports and physical activities evolving for many different reasons discussed earlier, forms of life also need to be able to adapt. If forms of life capturing athlete performance and development do not show some level of continued adaptation, then it could lead to system capture: that is, whole cohorts of athletes underachieving due to being locked in to traditional ways of performing, practicing and developing. Coaching and teaching in sport and physical activity programmes can be subjected to *system capture* when standard reference coaching manuals or talent development pathways do not evolve with trends in athlete development.

In ecological dynamics, the development of a *form of life* is emphasised, which leads to the design practice environments to encourage adaptability and resourcefulness of performers. Individual athletes who become attuned to relevant affordances are considered to have developed an *optimal grip* on *affordances,* underpinning the way that they can seize opportunities for action to express their autonomy and self-regulation in competitive sport.

An optimal grip on a field of affordances is founded on a functional relationship between cognition, perception and action of athletes when they are continuously challenged by sport practitioners to adapt to dynamic constraints of specific fields of an affordance landscape.

Summary

- The ideas presented in this section provide a conceptualised theoretical framework that is relevant for all athletes, irrespective of expertise, skill level or a specific sport.
- A theory to practice gap exists in sport science. Lots of complex interacting theoretical ideas can be confusing for sport practitioners. What they need to do is decide on a guiding theoretical framework that they can articulate to themselves or any informed observer of their work (not performers, unless in highly simplified terms).
- Frameworks can help to bridge the gap between theoretical understanding and practical application of ideas. A framework will act as a guidance tool for practitioners and researchers to ensure they are designing environments consistent with underpinning principles of ecological dynamics, in the case of CLA.
- The application of CLA in practice needs to be nuanced and continually evaluated.
- The overarching concept of the *individual–environment relationship* is a key principle to guide research and practice. Coaches need to consider the fit between the practice environment that they develop and the abilities of each individual learner and the capacities that are invited to emerge in each individual during practice. The manipulation of constraints is the main methodological aspect that a sport practitioner can use to design learning environments, regardless of skill level, expertise and experience of an athlete.
- Temporal nature of emerging and decaying constraints should dictate intentional constraints manipulation.
- Affordances or opportunities for action are *constraints* on athlete behaviours. These constraints can be designed into practice tasks.
- Sport practitioners are designers of affordances using the manipulation of constraints as a key methodology to enhance athlete performance and learning.
- However, the manipulation of constraints is a challenging task that requires careful consideration by a practitioner. It is not a magic bullet and practice task designs can be over-constraining, under-constraining or not relevant to a specific learner. The important questions to address in manipulating constraints include: Why? What? How? Who? and When?
- There is a need to avoid clichés like 'the game is teacher' because it fails to recognise the important active role of the coach in continuously manipulating different constraints at different times.

- The history of the individual shapes what emerges in learning: know the athlete's history so that practice tasks can build on what is already known and complement the athlete's current capacities.
- Transfer between practice and performance is important as a concept to get over to practitioners. Transfer can be specific or more general. There are benefits to both types of transfer. Specificity of transfer will support the most rapid learning. Generality of transfer will support the acquisition of skills that will enhance athletic performance more generally. Sport practitioners need to transition between both types of transfer, depending on the needs of each individual athlete.
- 'Will it transfer?' is the question that should guide evaluation of a practice task design to be implemented.
- Adding variability in learning contexts will help athletes become more flexible and adaptable in performance environments.
- The role of emotions as well as cognitions shapes perceptions and actions.
- An appreciation of the *form of life* is crucial for the provision of appropriate affordance landscapes to be searched by learners throughout their development.

Part II

A constraints-led approach

Building a bridge

5   The environment design principles

In the first three chapters we introduced the theoretical concepts of ecological dynamics to provide practitioners with the knowledge base to design effective CLA sessions. However, the key challenge for coaches is how to put these ideas into practice. To emphasise the key role that coaches play in the creation of effective practice environments, we proposed that coaches should see themselves as environment architects or learning designers. However, integrating complex theoretical ideas into learning design can be highly challenging as employing new ideas in practice can be a daunting and confusing task. It is this gap, between the theoretical underpinning and the practical application of a CLA, that is often cited as the most significant barrier coaches face as they negotiate the pragmatics of environmental design (Greenwood et al., 2014). The aim in this chapter is to address this issue, by introducing the Environment Design Principles (EDP). The EDP are provided as a potential solution to this problem, a bridge that practitioners can use to link the complex theoretical concepts in successful practical applications. Just like a bridge, the EDP are designed to support the practitioner's journey, providing a clear route between what would otherwise be two disconnected and distant locations (i.e. theory and practice). We hope that, through engagement with the four Environment Design Principles, coaches will feel more confident in exploring and adopting CLA into his or her practice. In summary, we propose that the EDP framework underpinned by the theoretical concepts of ED (Chow et al., 2016) discussed in Part I, will support a more nuanced understanding of CLA and enable practitioners to make more accurate and informed decisions in the design of practice environments. Ultimately, the provision of more innovative and robust practice environments is likely to facilitate a greater level of transferable and targeted skill development.

Environment Design Principles

The EDP operationalise the CLA by providing user-friendly principles to support coaches in the practice environment design process. The EDP consist of four principles that capture the core theoretical foundations of ecological dynamics (ED). The key principles are: (1) Session intention, (2) Constrain to afford, (3) Representative learning design (including purpose and consequence), and (4), Repetition without repetition (which is framed around manipulating variability to enhance adaptability and increase or decrease (in)stability). Each principle has its own unique purpose, resultantly impacting upon decisions a coach will make in the environment design process. While each principle is valuable in its own right, it is through the integration of all four principles that the framework is able operate effectively and efficiently. In this way, the EDP looks to support practitioner decision-making, as coaches engage in the messy process of practice design. We will introduce and unpack each principle throughout this chapter.

1. Session intention

Guiding principle: the intentions of the session act as an overriding and organisational constraint.

Principle 1 emphasises the role and importance of *session intention* in the environment design process. The intention of the session is an integral driver of coaches' decision making as they plan, prepare and deliver their practice environments. The importance of *intentions* and the impact they have on the interaction between performers and the landscape of affordances was introduced and explored in Chapter 3. As environment *designers* we need to appreciate that *intentions* do not just impact on our decision-making as coaches, but act as an over-riding constraint (*individual*) on performer and team cognitions. These, in turn, influence the perceptions and actions of performer(s) within a practice environment. Therefore, as a coach engages in the environment design process, it is critical that they establish the primary goal(s) (intentions) of the practice session as a first step. In practice, a coach has the opportunity to shape emergent behaviour through the application of a CLA. As previously indicated, the various constraints can be added, removed, adjusted or repositioned within the practice environment. This manipulation process is both complex and nuanced, requiring careful consideration, consideration that is governed by the *session intention*.

The goal of the practice environment can vary considerably for the coach and performer. For example, the intention of the session could be to learn a new skill, a cricket player developing a new shot to add to their repertoire, or a gymnast developing a new move on the beam. Alternatively, it may be the aim of the coach to improve players' tactical awareness while executing a zonal defensive system in soccer. The coach may wish to enhance the performer(s) collective understanding of counter-attack principles in an ice hockey context. Moreover, a coach may wish to develop the ability of his high jump performer(s) to cope and ultimately execute under extreme pressure. Or, perhaps, the intention of the session is to invite players to attune to the performance environment. In addition, with the increased input from sport science it is becoming increasingly common for practice environments to be specifically designed with the physical preparation of performers as the primary objective. For example, there is significant research on the use of small-sided games as a conditioning tool for soccer players (Hill-Haas et al., 2011). Moreover, the primary goal of the session could be to promote *learning*, therefore the practice environment needs to be designed to allow learners the opportunity to *explore*, *exploit* or *execute* solutions to the problem they have been set. As previously alluded to, coaches need to appreciate that *intentions* act as an over-riding constraint on performer and team cognitions, perceptions and actions. With this in mind, it is proposed that there must be an alignment between the intentions of the coach and the intentions of the learner(s). A disparity between a performer's intentions and a coach's desired actions can lead to failure and ultimately frustration for both the coach and the performer(s). It is therefore imperative that both performer and coach work to develop a shared understanding of the intention of the practice and the desirable intentions within the practice. We provide support for coaches by scaffolding this important process in Chapter 6.

The intentions of a practice session will be influenced by the *timing* of session. For example, if the session is in pre-season or in close proximity to a competitive performance, it will impact on the intention of the coach and the performer(s). While the development (and ultimately *learning*) of the performers should be at the forefront of the coach's long-term planning, it would not be prudent for a coach to *only* design and provide practice sessions that promote a re-organisation of the movement system. For example, it may not be advantageous to provide a session where learning is the primary objective the day before, or morning of, an important match or performance. The potential for an increased level of failure within these sessions (and associated performer frustration) could negatively impact on the competitive performance of the individual or team. Consistent with the example above, there may be practice environments in a performer's session, week or season where the primary goal will be performance preparation, where the performers *attune* to the performance environment by practising or rehearsing. For example, a tennis player may take to the court the morning of a game and rehearse by 'practising' against a partner, a rugby union team may participate in a 'team run' the day prior to competition, while it is common for a netball team to engage in a 'surface training' session in the lead-up to a competitive fixture.

It is integral that the intentions are matched to the needs of the performers. For example, a key consideration when setting session goals is a careful assessment of the current skill level of the learners. Appropriate knowledge of a learner's level is essential as it guides session focus and design. Current popular learning stage models include the three-stage models of Fitts and Posner (Cognitive, Associative, Autonomous) (1967) and Newell (Co-ordination, Control, Skill) (1985). Given that Fitts and Posner's model is underpinned and informed by an information-processing theory of motor learning, it does not fit theoretically with CLA, which is predicated on an ecological model of motor behaviour We are also of the belief that it is prudent for models to promote skill learning as the process of adapting or attuning to the environment, rather than viewing skill learning as a fixed outcome due to the connotations this promotes. The better fit for a CLA is therefore Newell's model. However, the terms used by Newell, particularly the use of the term 'skill' to describe the third stage of the model, can be confusing and not helpful in the application of CLA. To address this issue, Renshaw and Chow (2018) propose a two-stage adaptation of Newell's (1985) model. Stage 1 is a Learning to *Co-ordinate* phase and therefore this stage is about *searching* and *exploring* to develop intra-individual-environment or inter-individual-environment co-ordination patterns (Renshaw & Moy, 2018). Stage 2 builds on Stage 1 and assumes learners have developed basic co-ordination patterns enabling them to move into the *Adaptation* phase. This phase is concerned with optimising performance through developing stable, yet flexible, co-coordinative structures based on the emergent ability to *exploit* the individual–environment system (i.e. passive, inertial, and mechanical properties of limb movements (Davids et al., 2008). Session intentions and the subsequent learning design are therefore predicated on identifying the current needs of the performer, which are signposted by reference to the current stage of learning. Evaluation of current skill level should, therefore, be undertaken in advance of session design. Or if this is the first session with an individual or team, the first task may be used as an assessment. Here, it might be helpful to view the initial activity as a 'pre-test' that provides the baseline for current skill level and informs session goals. We build on this point in the next chapter using an adapted version of the GROW model (Whitmore, 2017).

2. Constrain to afford

Guiding principle: 'design-in' constraints to offer/invite/encourage learners to explore the opportunities for action related to the session intention.

Principle 2 brings together the concepts of constraints and affordances, challenging coaches to manipulate constraints to systematically design-in affordances to the practice environment. This principle builds on the discussion of affordances presented to the reader in Chapters 3 and 4 by operationalising them for coaches. Given that skill learning is predicated on performers learning to adapt to the environment through attunement to, and exploitation of, key affordances in that environment, it is a key requirement of constraint-led coaching to design practice environments that specifically provide opportunities for performers to become more attuned or adapted to the performance environment (Araújo & Davids, 2011a). However, it is common that performers are unable to 'pick up' the key affordances and coaches need to direct their performers search by using constraints that emphasise or exaggerate the presence of available affordances. This process is called *constraining to afford*. Essentially, this approach requires practitioners to design-in constraints that will make available desired affordances in a practice task, channelling the performer towards their availability in the landscape (Chow et al., 2016). It makes sense that the initial step for coaches is to *offer* the important affordances that are relevant to the session *intention*. Designing learning tasks through the manipulation of constraints to provide affordances for action requires practitioners to be 'problem setters' who are able to implicitly invite functional perception–action couplings. For example, if a squash player wishes to develop the ability to execute an effective drop shot, the environment must be designed to both *offer* (provide lots of opportunities) and *invite* (create the need for) the player to perform the drop shot. The notion of constrain to afford postulates that the decisions to act need to come via performers *choosing* and not being *forced* to attune to the affordances in the environment. It is vital to consider that the decision about when to act is as important as the action itself and the two must remain coupled to the performance environment. Indeed, just because an affordance is available does not mean an individual performer should use it; in fact, knowing when a player 'ought' to use an available affordance is perhaps just as important as knowing how to use it (Heft, 2003). These ideas are aligned with the suggested re-definition of affordances as 'invitations for action' proposed by Withagen et al. (2012, 2017).

In simple terms, well-structured environment design must offer performers the opportunity to move beyond 'what' they must do, and towards an understanding that allows them to construct for themselves the 'how, why, where and when' of movement in sport performance. In practice, helping performers to learn to recognise the affordances, when, why and ultimately how to use them, requires sampling of 'the landscape of affordances' from performance, and ensuring that the most important affordances are available in practice. Chapter 4 introduced and provided readers with a discussion of the affordance landscape. It is essential that the practice environment not only provides the performers with opportunities to attune to a range of possible affordances but solicits (invites) those actions. A useful strategy to aid this process is adopting the principles of exaggeration (see Renshaw et al., 2015; Bunker & Thorpe, 1982). For example, a badminton coach may use a long thin court to encourage the learner to recognise when the space is in front of or behind the opponent. This principle calls for practitioners to manipulate practice environments to encourage performers to engage with available affordances in a more effective and efficient manner as they self-organise to solve the problem presented. An additional example of this principle in action is the use of a *taped* (tennis) ball in cricket to *offer* (*invite*) the batter the opportunity to bat against a swinging ball. We explore in-depth examples of how a coach can adapt their environments to meet this principle in our Constraints in Action chapters located later in the book (Part III).

3. Representative learning design

Guiding principle: ensure that what the learners are seeing, hearing and feeling in the practice environment is similar to the performance environment.

Principle 3 requires coaches to consider the impact that *representative design* has on learning transfer. One of the most important concerns for coaches who are interested in improving performance is the degree to which what one learns in 'practice' transfers to the competitive environment. Representative learning design (RLD) was introduced in Chapter 2 and developed as a principle to focus coaches' thinking by requiring them to sample the performance environment and ensure that practice and training task constraints are representative of a particular sport performance context (Chow et al., 2011; Pinder et al., 2011). Egon Brunswik (1955) termed this environmental feature: *representative design*. Paying attention to the principle of RLD ensures that learning tasks contain relevant informational constraints to elicit the emergence of functional behaviours and facilitates attunement to key affordances (Fajen et al., 2009). The importance of promoting the development of functional behaviours in practice (i.e. those that are effective and efficient in performance) is captured in representative task design (Brunswik, 1955) as the concept advocates the need to maintain action-fidelity (Stoffregen et al., 2003). Consequently, coaches need to sample practice environments to ensure that they have similar information flows to a performance environment, making them more representative and maintaining greater action-fidelity. In simple terms, action fidelity promotes the idea that a coach must ensure that the movement solutions the performers exhibit and develop in the practice environment will be effective when transferred to the performance environment. For example, learning to shoot without defenders in a basketball context has the potential to develop an ineffective movement solution when transferred to the performance environment (Gorman & Maloney, 2017). The concept of RLD calls into question the value of practice task designs that are de-contextualised through the provision of overly artificial information sources and task decomposition. As a result, these design faults may potentially inhibit the coupling of perception and action systems during task performance. This element builds on the concept of perception–action coupling presented in Chapter 2. To exemplify, in practical learning interventions, it is important to avoid designing an environment that requires performers to dribble around cones or manikins – with the intention of creating realism in ball manipulation practice. Without information from movements and locations of opposing defenders, spatial (line markings) or temporal (tempo of a ball feed) informational constraints, to exemplify, there will be little strengthening of the functional perception–action couplings required in skilled performance (see Chapter 3 for empirical research studies that support these ideas). This type of practice task design is inefficient and ineffective for all but the most novice learners, and even for that group the shelf-life of cone dribbling is limited. The limitations of this type of design exemplify practice opportunities that do not include specifying information, which can be used to regulate action. Renshaw et al. (2007) demonstrated that batting against bowling machines as opposed to real bowlers led to a re-organisation of the timing and co-ordination of a forward defensive shot and did not facilitate opportunities for batters to learn to utilise information from the bowler's actions, a key component of expert batting performance (Müller et al., 2006). We also described an example of the limitations of ball machines in Chapter 2. We suggest that RLD embedded in a CLA allows practitioners to design experiences during practice that are more likely to have a significant impact on learning (and therefore enhance performance). A focus on learning to adapt or attune to the landscape of affordances available in performance environments, changes the focus of practice from rehearsal and the memorisation of putatively 'perfect' techniques (via the ubiquitous use of isolated drills), towards the engagement in functional and contextually relevant interactions. The change in emphasis from *actions* to *interactions* is an important idea in an ecological dynamics rationale for skill adaptation; the latter captures the intertwined nature of intentions, perception and action in goal-directed behaviour.

To advance these ideas of RLD further, and highlight the interaction between emotions, intentions, perceptions and actions, the concept of Affective Learning Design (Headrick et al., 2015) was developed. In simple terms, by adopting ALD, practitioners can check the representativeness of practice session by asking 'does the practice look *and feel* similar to the real thing?' Essential to this design process is ensuring that the task outcome has been given a purposeful intention and that there are clear consequences of success or failure emerging from interactions of athletes with the environment. A failure to ensure this aspect of RLD may lead to athletes 'going through the motions' and performing below competition intensity. Consequently, this type of practice design creates similar intentions, emotions and emergent perception–action couplings to those seen in performance context (Maloney et al., 2018).

A pause to gather your thoughts: *With great power comes great responsibility* – we urge coaches to be mindful and perhaps cautious of the re-organisation their practice environments are shaping. It is paramount that the self-organising process facilitates a re-organisation that will be advantageous to the player when transferred to the performance environment. For example, in soccer, placing cones on the floor for players to dribble around could promote the development of a solution where a player's vision is directed at the ground rather than scanning the pitch. It could be argued that this would not be a functional fit and is therefore not of any use to the player in the game where there is a need to scan while in possession of the ball. In this example it is important to remember who placed the cones on the ground in the first place before becoming frustrated with a player's movement solutions!

4. Repetition without repetition (including variability and in(stability))

Guiding principle: 'design-in' the appropriate amount of variability and (in)stability to the practice environment.

Principle 4 considers the concept of practice variability and requires coaches to manage how much variability they should design-in to the practice environment. Whereas much of the previous work in skill acquisition has focused on task variability (i.e. blocked versus random practice or contextual interference), variability in CLA promotes coaches to also consider and adjust the environmental variability with the aim of providing an appropriate level of (in)stability for performers.

A key feature common across sport is the belief of practitioners that we become 'skilled' by doing repetition after repetition. However, evidence in motor behaviour research has highlighted that repeating the same movement over and over again is an impossibility (Bernstein, 1967) and that variable practice is more advantageous to skill learning (Magill & Hall, 1990). Consequently, Bernstein suggested embracing repetition without repetition, thereby providing environments that allow performers to undertake lots of repetitions of achieving the same outcomes in different ways. He proposed that 'Practice is a particular type of repetition without repetition' (Bernstein, 1967, p. 134), and strongly advocated against a type of practice that is 'merely mechanical repetition by rote', which had already been

Figure 5.1 1 vs 1 shooting/dribbling practices in field hockey are 'fed' by the coach with players rotating their receiving positions to create repetition of practice, without repetition.

discredited in his opinion. In designing 'repetition without repetition' in practice, performers are provided with opportunities to search and explore to create a range of effective and adaptable movement solutions. Essentially, Bernstein highlighted the need for flexibility in skill development to encourage learners to seek different solutions to the same or similar problems. This principle builds on Chapter 2 where we introduce the concepts of dexterity, degeneracy and repetition without repetition.

Building repetition without repetition into practice is essential in dynamic, complex environments such as sports. For example, in a field hockey game, no two passes are ever identical as the position of team members, opponents, the state of the game, the surface, the time and space available to make a pass, are never the same. Consequently, practice must offer the player lots of opportunities to pass the ball over different distances, in different directions and at different speeds to different team members or to different places for the same receiver. Players must be given opportunities to learn to adapt their hitting co-ordination patterns to cope in many different dynamic situations (see Button et al., 2006). Similarly, in an individual sport like swimming, adaptability is crucial for success and repetition without repetition is a key factor in its emergence. For example, if one was to consider the swimmer who was the best in their state, the majority of their competitive swimming would be undertaken in the centre lanes (the fastest swimmers are allocated the centre lanes in races). It is also most likely that the swimmer is often leading the race and does not have to deal with the wake created by swimmers being ahead of them. Indeed, in the past swimmers have exploited the wake of leading swimmers (see A pause to gather your thoughts, below). However, once the swimmer enters higher-level competitions the chances are that they will be required to swim in the outside lanes next to the walls. It makes sense therefore that swimmers should be prepared for competition by swimming in different lanes and through careful handicapping swimmers could practise 'chasing' opponents as well as leading. It would also help prepare swimmers for situations such as being last off the blocks in a short race and hence knowing how best to pace the race. Of course, the added advantage of adding variability like this, is that the swimmer has more opportunity to learn to embrace and exploit the tactical and psychological impact of different race scenarios (see the discussion of ALD above).

A pause to gather your thoughts: At the 1984 Summer Olympics, a 17-year-old Brisbane boy, Jon Seiben, competed in the 200 m butterfly. As a novice and due to his diminutive (175 cm) stature for an elite swimmer (Seiben was known as the Shrimp), he was seen as a rank outsider and given no chance of winning any colour of medal, let alone a gold. Seiben's challenge was indeed a steep one, given he

(continued)

(continued)

was up against the legendary Michael Gross, the world record holder, who was known as *The Albatross* given his 200 cm height and 225 cm wingspan. He also faced the 100-metre butterfly world record holder, Pablo Morales of the United States. However, Seiben and his coach, Laurie Lawrence, had a plan. They decided to swim in the wake of Gross and Morales in the first 150 metres and then attack in the last lap. The strategy worked a treat and Seiben stunned the swimming world, claiming the gold medal in a world record time of 1 m 57.04 s, more than four seconds faster than he had ever swum before.

The previous examples highlight that, practically, coaches can adjust the amount of variability within the practice environment through the manipulation of individual (e.g. intentions, optimising strategy to match the intrinsic dynamics), environmental (e.g. different opponents, surfaces or water conditions) or task constraints (e.g. different competition scenarios, or pitch sizes). The key question for coaches is how much variability to design-in to the practice environment for each performer or group of athletes. Additionally, coaches need to decide whether they are going to control the amount of variability through the systematic or random manipulation of constraints. Orth et al. (2018) addressed these challenges, suggesting that practitioners can utilise systematic and unsystematic approaches by the manipulation of constraints (Ranganathan & Newell, 2013). The unsystematic manipulation of constraints involves practitioners constantly and randomly manipulating task and environmental constraints, for example, randomly changing racquet sizes or ball types when teaching tennis (Lee et al., 2014).

The amount of variability designed into a session needs to be matched to the performer's current level of skill. For the beginner level player who is at the co-ordination stage, low-task and environmental variability may be initially beneficial to guide exploration towards one or two functional solutions. In contrast, the more expert performer, who is at Stage 2 (the adaptability level), may be presented with greater variability in individual, task and environmental constraints to promote more dexterous behaviour. Rosser (2008) discussed the notion that complex systems (i.e. human beings or teams) are open to (in)stabilities, exhibit complex chaotic behaviour, and that, in attempts to self-organise against these fluctuations, the process of pattern-formation (system re-organisation) takes place. Put simply, the learners in the practice environment will endeavour to make sense (self-organise) of the chaos (instability) they are presented with by forming functional action solutions. This leads us to the purposeful manipulation of control parameters (via task constraints) in the aim of deliberately moving performers into less stable areas to promote a re-organisation of the movement system (Handford et al., 1997). When designing practices for learning, it is essential that coaches manipulate the system to be poised at the critical point, *on the edge of chaos* (Bowes & Jones, 2006). Knowledge of 'critical values' (i.e. the amount of variability that will lead to instability and the search for new solutions) is important for coaches and requires careful management and awareness of the implications for placing individuals in these critical zones (see Chapter 6). This tipping point on the edge of chaos is often the location of the optimum instability for the performer(s) (we describe this as the amber zone in the next chapter). On the other hand, sometimes it is advantageous for a coach to design-in a low amount of variability, as he or she may wish to design practice tasks that do not promote any additional pattern forming or system re-organisation (we describe this as the green zone in the next chapter). In contrast, there will be a 'critical value' above which the environment will contain too much variability and as a result will become inherently chaotic and unmanageable (we present this as the red zone in the next chapter) (Davids, 2003). The manipulation of *task* constraints such as the lane in which a swimmer must race, the score and time left in a combat fight or the number of learners, size and shape of the playing area, number of objects, and equipment scaling in a team sport, will all have significant impact on the amount of information to which performers are required to attend. For example, if a novice performer is placed into a practice environment with a large number of opponents and teammates with a multitude of performance solutions, the environment could become too difficult to perceive and act upon. For some performers, this type of practice task design could contain information overload. In this case, the manipulation of *task* constraints (e.g. a reduction in the number of opponents and teammates), to reduce the amount of variability, has the potential for better engagement and development of the performers, at a specific stage of learning and development. In summary, individual performers need to be provided with practice task constraints that allow them to explore dexterity in their interactions with the performance environment. The affordances explored during learning need to be well-considered and fit completely with the effectivities of the performers in the group. Essential to this process is the appropriate provision of variability and (in)stability in the practice environment.

The generation of functionally variable movement patterns is an important characteristic of skilled performers operating within a dynamic environment. The importance of this variability was emphasised in Chapter 2 where we introduced the concepts of 'dexterity' and 'degeneracy' (Bernstein, 1967, p. 228). We propose designing-in the appropriate level of variability to the practice environment will align the practice environment with the repetition without repetition principle, thus facilitating the development of performers with a greater ability to organising their body in many different ways to solve any emerging motor problem correctly, quickly, rationally and resourcefully. As a result, a coach must manipulate task constraints in practice environments to offer both repetition and variation (i.e. repetition without repetition) to facilitate this process (Travassos et al., 2012).

Summary

In summary, the *Environment Design Principles* (EDP) provide a framework to guide coaches as they navigate the complex and nuanced process of practice design. The four distinct principles provide coaches with the tools required to bridge the gap between the theoretical underpinning and the successful application of a CLA. Coaches should endeavour to meet the four guiding principles by attending to the following elements throughout the design, adaptation and delivery of their practice environments:

1   *Session intention*

- Employ a clearly established session intention as an organisational constraint as you design your session.
- Ensure that session intention is aligned with the intentions of your performers.
- Consider the timing of your session alongside the needs of the performers when establishing the session intention.

2   *Constrain to afford*

- View yourself as a 'problem setter' who designs practice sessions to facilitate implicit skill development.
- Manipulate constraints to design-in specific affordances for performers to engage with in your practice landscape.
- Avoid 'over constraining' to *force* and instead aim to *invite* engagement with specific affordances through a process of exaggeration.

3   *Representative learning design*

- To maximise the potential for learning transfer ensure you consider the impact of representative design.
- Use task simplification rather than task decomposition to ensure higher levels of RLD.
- Design-in RLD to your practice environment by ensuring that perception–action remain coupled.
- Ensure you have considered amplitude of ALD in the design of your practice environment.

4   *Repetition without repetition*

- Encourage the development of dexterity by ensuring with repetition without repetition rather than repetition after repetition is evident in the practice environment.
- Determine the appropriate amount of variability to match the current abilities of the performers.

- Decide if the variability is to be systematically or randomly designed-in to your practice environment.
- Deliberately design-in a period of (in)stability for your performers by adjusting the amount of variability within your practice environment.

The following chapter (6) provides coaches with a stage-like model, scaffolding the coach through the process of designing and adjusting their practice environments, supporting the application of these complex ideas into their practice.

6 The constraints-led approach
Session designer

The aim of this chapter is to provide guidelines to implement the four principles discussed previously into the design of a CLA session. We will provide a step-by-step planning framework that will enable a coach to build his or her own CLA sessions. As part of this approach we will introduce new resources that coaches can use and provide some ideas to enable the consideration of the level of representativeness of practice and deliberate designing-in of affordances, variability, and instability. We will introduce representative learning design (RLD) and variability 'dials', which require coaches to pay attention to these core ideas in their session design and provide a tool that coaches can use to systemically manipulate constraints. We will conclude by providing a debriefing template to emphasise that adopting a CLA is a dynamic, iterative process where the coach and performer coach create an emergent learning and performance programme. We begin by adopting the ideas of the GROW model (Whitmore, 2017) to pose a series of questions that can form the foundation for CLA learning design.

Planning a CLA session

Step one: the current landscape

When designing any session, it is important to understand the current landscape for the performer(s). This requires collecting as much information as possible about the individual(s) and the performance environment. In line with Principle 1 introduced in the previous chapter, we have adapted Whitmore's (2017) GROW model to frame this process. GROW is an acronym to describe a process that involves four key steps. Goal: what do you want? Reality: where are you now? Option: what could you do? Will: what will you do? In our adaptation, we have used *Way Forward* to replace 'Will' as we wanted to emphasise that this process is in line with our goal in this book, to move coaching forward and provide new alternative ways to frame coaching practice. As such, it is important to recognise the link between the GROW questions to the how, what, why and when (and whom) questions we raised in the earlier discussion. Adopting this more systematic approach

CONSTRAINT-LED SESSION PLANNING

G GOAL	R REALITY	O OPTIONS	W WAY FORWARD

• What's the goal or intention for this session?
• How does this link to the overall goal?
• The focus for learning is . . .?
	• What's the current skill level?
	   ○ Co-ordination?
	   ○ Adaptability?
	• What affordances of the performance environment do you want to design-in to practice?
	   ○ Which?
	   ○ Why?
	   ○ When?
		• What practice activities will bridge the gap?
		• Which practice environment will you use?
		• What constraints will you use and how will you manipulate them?
		• How will you measure performance?
		• We will know we have been successful if:
		   ○ We can see . . .
		   ○ The data shows . . .
		   ○ The coach says . . .
		   ○ The performer feels . . .
			• How will you prepare the practice environment?
			• How will you prepare the performers for the session?
			• Is there anything else you need to do to be ready?

Figure 6.1 Adapted GROW model for constraints-led session planning.

to CLA session design highlights how constraints-led coaching can be much more nuanced than simply adding in different rules seen when using SSCGs, for example. As shown in Figure 6.1, we have used GROW and added questions that frame it a CLA to coaching.

Goal

What is the goal or intention for this session?

Unless this is the first session a coach is going to run with an individual or team, he or she should have a pretty good idea of what needs to be worked on in this session. Ideally, this decision should be informed by some form of performance analysis, which may be as simple as watching how they performed, or at higher levels based on some form of data analysis. It is important that the goals or intentions of the coach are matched with those of the performers. As highlighted in previous chapters, a mis-match between what coaches want to see and what the performers can do can lead to frustration and failure for the coach and performer. Just because the coach wants to see the performer reproduce the perfect movement model shown in coaching books, does not mean that they have the current capability to achieve this desired goal and repeated attempts that lead to failure may have a detrimental effect and lead to negative consequences such as lower confidence, reduced interest and, ultimately, decreased motivation. Consequently, apart from with very young performers, a joint approach to session design is recommended to ensure that there is buy-in from the performers. This does not mean that everyone should sit down and plan the detail of session together (which, of course, they could do), but it does mean that the coach should at least talk to the performers to get their views as to the key areas to focus on moving forward. In elite sport this process might take place in the post-match review, with the coach using the feedback to determine the goals for the session.

How does this link to the overall goal?

In this book we are assuming that the coaching is geared towards improving performance and that the individual sport performer or team are taking part in or preparing for some sort of competitive programme. Consequently, the coach and performers should be working towards an overall goal. These goals can be short (e.g. to win the next competition, to qualify for a tournament), medium (e.g. to be selected for a representative squad) or long-term (e.g. to become a professional performer). The session that is being planned should, therefore, sit in a connected space (i.e. practice design and competition performances should be linked) and form part of a process of attempting to achieve an overall goal. It is worth noting that this does not imply that the overall plan needs to be rigid and fixed a long time in advance (i.e. a detailed, session-by-session, periodised plan). Rather, each session's goals need to emerge as the performer progresses (or not). Of course, this includes within as well as between sessions. This is comparable to planning a journey; we know the destination and what time we must arrive by. We may have a rough idea of the options available to get us to the destination, but actual decisions about which road to take at a point in time might change in the moment due to local conditions. In our coaching, this means that we are adaptable and flexible in the design of our overall programme and even in defining the ultimate overall goal.

The focus for learning is . . .

Once the goal for the session is determined, it is useful to summarise what the focus of learning is going to be for the session. The focus of learning is on closing the gap between the current skill level and the level required to succeed. Essentially, this means identifying the most relevant 'rate limiter' (i.e. the key factors that are acting as a handbrake) on the emergence of higher levels of performance. Traditionally, the term 'rate limiter' is associated with motor development and is typically used to describe how the relatively slower rate of development of a specific subsystem can act to prevent a new behaviour from emerging. For example, a lack of strength can delay the onset of walking in babies (Thelen & Smith, 1994). In sport coaching these ideas can be broadened to include environmental and task constraints such as limited opportunities to practise in specific performance settings or against highly skilled opponents. Of course, given the above definition, the focus of a session can relate to any aspect of performance and could involve a specific focus on individual skills, team co-ordination, emotional control, perceptual skills and so on. It is worth noting, that while the session will have a specific focus for learning, the interactive nature of constraints will likely result in some other expected and perhaps unexpected learnings that coaches could exploit in their practice.

Reality

What is the current skill level?

- Co-ordination?
- Adaptability?

As mentioned previously, the goals and intentions of the coach need to be matched to those of the performers. Therefore, a careful assessment of the current skill level of the performers is required to ensure alignment to the goals set for the session. Recently, in an attempt to provide a more workable categorisation of skill level for teachers and coaches, Renshaw and Chow (2018) proposed an adaptation of Newell's (1985) three-stage learning model (Co-ordination, Control, Skill) (see box below).

Key concept: Newell's (1985) skill framework

Stage 1: Co-ordination. Is focussed on the assembly of a suitable, functional (i.e. it works) coordination pattern.

Stage 2: Control: This phase is concerned with building on the established co-ordination patterns to enable greater attunement to dynamic performance environments. Gaining control of the co-ordination pattern is therefore typically characterized by subtle, refined variations in movement patterning to strengthen its adaptability

(continued)

(continued)

in different circumstances, allowing them to function more adaptively in many situations (Liu, Mayer-Kress, & Newell, 2006).

Stage 3: Skill: The final stage of Newell's (1985) model refers to the optimization of skill. Essentially, this means gaining even more control of the coordinative structure through the learned ability to exploit intrinsic dynamics and more flexible and open to exploit environmental information sources. Performers therefore become more flexible, efficient and have increased control as they become adept at exploiting forces from the movement, including instantaneous adaptations to sudden and minute environmental changes (Newell, 1996).

A more complete review of Newell's (1985) framework and the ideas behind can be found in the original paper and in Davids et al. (2008).

Describing a performer as being at 'Skill' level was felt to be confusing and not helpful when talking to practitioners about skill learning. Additionally, as highlighted by Newell himself (1985), the framework only fits well with discrete (e.g. hitting a ball, throwing an implement) and serial tasks (e.g. a gymnastics tumbling routine, penalty flick in field hockey) and not continuous tasks (e.g. running, swimming, cycling) where strategy 'over rides any single aspect of individual co-ordination within the context of the activity (p. 296). Given the focus on developing flexibility and adaptability in the second and third stages, Renshaw and Chow (2018) reduced Newell's model to two stages. Stage 1 was categorised as a *Learning to Co-ordinate* phase (as per Newell) with a second stage being classed as a *Learning to Adapt* phase (a collapsing of Control and Skill from Newell's model).

In reality, the age, experience and standard of competition (i.e. international, national, 5th Division), may lead coaches to assume the current skill levels of their performers; however, it is still worth the coach paying particular attention to each individual performer's status, particularly in sports where there are a range of skills that need to be utilised (e.g. backhand and forehand shots in racquet sports, creating different flight characteristics in golf, or kicking a ball with both feet and different surfaces in football). As many coaches understand, in any squad or team, performers are at different stages and levels in their development. Additionally, a performer may be at the adaptable stage in some skills, but still at co-ordination level in others. Unfortunately (in our experience and opinion), a lack of understanding of the stage of learning leads many coaches to only focus on the co-ordination stage. Hence, even with elite performers, coaching is often focused on breaking down deeply learned complex moment patterns in attempts to re-model the co-ordination pattern. While at times this may be necessary, it has significant consequences for performance and the psychological state of the individual. We would caution such a focus and suggest that coaching time might be more effectively spent helping the performer to become more adaptable in their performance. For those at Stage 1, session goals should be more about creating learning opportunities that promote *searching* and *exploring* to facilitate the development of intra-individual-environment or inter-individual-environment co-ordination patterns (Renshaw & Moy, 2018). Those performers who have developed basic co-ordination patterns move into the Adaptation Phase. This phase is concerned with optimising performance through developing stable, yet flexible, co-ordination patterns based on the emergent ability to *exploit* affordances available in the individual-environment system (i.e. passive, inertial, and mechanical properties of limb movements (Renshaw & Chow, 2018; Davids et al., 2008). Essential to this process is providing learning opportunities to educate; (i) intentions (the process of setting up the perceptual or perceptual-motor systems to detect a particular informational variable), (ii) attention (the process of coming to attend to the more useful variables) and to calibrate actions of performers (the process by which the single-valued function itself becomes adjusted). Attention is said to be optimally educated if perceivers detect a variable that specifies the property that they intend to perceive (Jacobs & Michaels, 2007). To support this goal, learning environments must be highly representative of the performance environment in order to create high levels of transfer in terms of knowing what to do and how to do it in specific situations. Ensuring that session design has a high level of RLD has the potential to result in greater adaptability as performers are able to demonstrate an ability to adapt to, and ultimately instantly exploit, minute environmental changes leading to greater smoothness and fluidity in movements (Davids et al., 2008; Newell, 1996).

What affordances of the performance environment do you want to design-in to practice?

- Which?
- Why?
- When?

Once the stage of learning of the performers has been determined, specific decisions can be made about the design of the learning environment. Of particular relevance is deciding which affordances need to be designed-in, knowing why they should (or should not) be available and when they should be included in practice task design. For example, if a four-year-old child is learning to hit a tennis ball with mum or dad, the key affordance that needs to be provided is balls thrown to him or her on the bounce at an appropriate pace and in a place to invite swinging a racquet at. In contrast, a performance-level tennis player who is learning when to play a passing shot or a lob, needs the affordance of an opponent who is charging the net and inviting a return hit into the space either to the side or behind. Clearly, the decision as to when to design-in this affordance is determined by need, that is, when being able to execute passing shots and lobs becomes a significant requirement for success.

Option

What PRACTICE ACTIVITIES will bridge the gap?

Sport coaches will have a range of practice activities available to them to create learning environments that meet the goals of the session. The skill of coaching is identifying which activity is best matched to the needs of the performers. The traditional coaching session typically follows the same format. That is, a warm-up (usually non-related to the goals of the session), a decontextualised technical practice, followed by a generic game with a concluding non-related warm-down. The majority of these sessions result in the development of skills and abilities that lead to minimal transfer to the performance environment. We need to move away from this formulaic approach to choose tasks that will result in effective transfer. Coaches need to design sessions that spend the majority of time undertaking learning activities that improve performance effectively and efficiently. Our goal is to support this process.

Which PRACTICE ENVIRONMENT will you use?

Where a coach can run a practice session is a key constraint that impacts the design of coaching sessions. Learning and practice settings can include using the actual performance environment (completely, parts of and with or without modifications) as well as 'other' venues. It is important for the coach to identify all possible options and make informed decisions when designing the learning environment. Figure 6.2 provides an example of an environment selector for golf. This figure shows that the golf coach may be able to choose from a range of possible 'off-course' options such as the driving range, a putting green, a short game area, an indoor trackman 'room' or virtual golf simulator. Alternately, on-course options may be available, which might include the 'competition venue', similar courses, par three courses or just 'courses'. A key decision for the coach is how important the representativeness of the environment is to meet the session goals. This can be understood with reference to the concept of affordances discussed above and in the theoretical chapters. The coach may therefore 'slide' up and down the 'level of representativeness continuum within sessions.

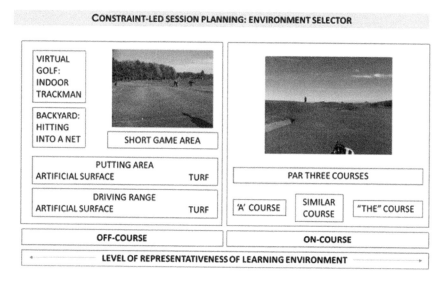

Figure 6.2 An example of an environment selector for golf.

What constraints will you use and how will you manipulate them?

A primary requirement when implementing a CLA is to identify all possible constraints that can influence performance. To this end, we suggest that coaches should formulate their own table of constraints by separating them into individual (and team), environmental and task constraints (see Chapter 3). Once a comprehensive list has been created then the coach can design-in the 'constraints to afford' that will help meet the session intentions. Ideally, the choice of constraint is based on an understanding of its likely impact on performance. That is, we can use a constraint as a control parameter (see theoretical chapters) to create a re-organisation of co-ordination or use a range of 'random' constraints (e.g. different types and sizes of tennis racquets, different ball types in invasion games) to encourage exploration to solve task problems. However, given that empirical research on specific examples of control parameters or the effectiveness of adding in random constraints in specific sports is still rare, it is often up to the coach to use his or her experiential knowledge or intuitive thinking to select which constraints to design-in. The next key decision is when to add in the constraint, how long to leave it in for, or when to manipulate it, with the caveat of knowing 'how much' to manipulate it by. For example, a long jump coach who wants to improve an athlete's vertical impulse at take-off may place a small hurdle 1 m in front of the take-off board that requires a higher knee lift to get over. Once the athlete has got this 'feeling' then the hurdle could be removed. The coach would then check that the 'new' behaviour was

THE CONSTRAINTS BUILDER FOR GOLF

INDIVIDUAL	ENVIRONMENT	TASK
Power	Surface Hardness	Competition Type
Fatigue	Grass Characteristics	Scoring System
Emotions	Wind	Competition Score
Intentions	Climate	Competition Position
Playing Style	Temperature	Clubs to Use
Confidence	Rain	Ball Types
	Green Speeds	Course Length
	Course Contours	Bunker Heights
	Course Location	Sand Type in Bunkers
	Club Culture	Additional Rules
	Opponents—Friendly	Mulligans
	Opponents—Aggressive	Reverse Mulligans
	Sledging	Speed Golf
	Caddies	

Figure 6.3 An example of a constraints builder for golf.

being maintained after the hurdle had been removed. This is an important point for all coaches, as any artificially 'added' constraint that is not present in the performance acts as an affordance to shape behaviour. We, therefore, should only leave the constraint in place long enough to create an established co-ordination pattern. Of course, this length of time may vary from individual to individual, but coaches will become better at making decisions about how long to leave a constraint in place through experiential knowledge. As such, choosing which constraints to use, how much to manipulate them by and how long to leave them in place is an exploratory learning process for the coach in the same way as we are encouraging in the performer.

How will you measure performance?

An often-overlooked aspect of coaching behaviour during practice is systematically and objectively measuring performance to move beyond the often-used intuitional level of 'gut feel' of the coach. What to measure is determined by the goals that are decided by coach and athlete(s). While many coaches below elite levels may not have access to support staff such as performance analysts, biomechanists, conditioning staff and sport psychologists who can objectively collect data, access to modern technologies (e.g. tablets, smart phones, drones) give the everyday coach access to ways of recording athlete behaviours and responses to session design. Additionally, injured players or parents can be asked to help. A good way to frame performance related to the set goals is to decide in advance of the session what a 'successful' outcome looks like. The following question frames this idea.

We will know we have been successful if

- We see . . .
- The data shows . . .
- The coach says . . .
- The performer feels . . .

To ascertain whether a coaching intervention has had any observable effect, a baseline is needed, preferably over a number of competitions, to ensure that a poor (or good) performance or sub-component was truly reflective of

Table 6.1 Exemplar for 'success' measures in CLA

	Individual sports	*Team sports*
We see . . .	an improvement in the number of serves landing in the tennis/volleyball/ badminton court	that the team created much greater space when on the ball by using the full width of the field and stretching the distance between the forwards and backs
We see . . .	the body language of the learner remains positive after a mistake has been made	an increase our defensive intensity immediately after we score
The data show . . .	that the judo player dominated the centre of the mat for 75% of the fight	a 10% increase in the number of times the ball enters the opponent's defensive zone within 5 seconds after a turnover
The data show . . .	80% of golf greens were hit in regulation;	our defensive wide players reduced the number of crosses by 20%
The coach says . . .	the sound of the footfalls in the run-up told me he was attacking the take-off board with good rhythm today	we reacted in a much more positive way after we made a mistake
The coach says . . .	the 800 m athlete maintained a good body shape in the last 50 m	
The performer(s) feel(s) . . .	much more confident in making solid returns when the ball is hit to my back hand side	
The performer(s) feel(s) . . .	much smoother in the water due to practicing in the wake of another swimmer	that they are playing with much more intensity due to their improved fitness

the 'norm' for performance. Determining in advance what is defined as 'success' in terms of a coaching intervention is necessary and can be framed in terms of 'we see . . .', 'the data shows . . .', 'the coach says . . .', 'the performer feels . . .' Table 6.1 provides some exemplar examples to illustrate these ideas.

It is worth cautioning here, that development is nonlinear and just because instant qualitative or quantitative changes cannot be observed, it does not mean that some learning has not taken place. Often coaches, need to be persistent but also patient in pursuing goals.

Way forward

Use of instructional constraints

How will you prepare the practice environment?

While still important, preparing the practice environment involves more than just setting out the equipment, writing up the session outline on the white board and paying overall attention to the mechanics of the session. It also refers to the creation of the cultural and social environment (cf. with the form of life as discussed in Chapter 4) that is developed and sustained by the coaching and support staff, and which athletes 'buy into'. It is essential that coaches and support staff view themselves as a key part of the practice environment and recognise the significant impact of their communications (both verbal and non-verbal). It is, therefore, important for the coach to plan what to say at key moments of the session and to anticipate the likely reactions of individuals in response to coaching interventions. The coach should therefore carefully plan the language used and ensure the expectations, values and beliefs of the session are clear. An additional consideration for elite coaches who may have a coaching and support team is the significant danger that the messages given to the players are not consistent. The head coach must ensure that everyone is 'singing from the same hymn sheet'.

How will you prepare the performers for the session?

An important consideration is how the coach will prepare the player's mentally and physically in advance of the session, emphasising the intertwined relationship between cognitions, intentions perceptions and actions (see Chapter 2). To maximise the impact of the session, performers may need to be primed in terms of framing the task in the context of the bigger picture. That is, by framing and setting intentions and clarifying expectations. For example, it is essential that the performers are made aware if the main intention of the session is learning or performing. This links to creating a climate where 'mistakes' are framed as being part of a process of exploration and the overall goal of developing adaptability, or where the goal is clinical execution. Consequently, coaches may use pre-practice meetings with teams and individuals accompanied by the production of materials to support the delivery of the session. For example, highlights packages of previous competition footage, short notes to individuals, or perhaps referrals could be made to other media (e.g. podcasts, interviews and online videos). Overall, the coach needs to know that the performers are totally prepared for the upcoming session.

Is there anything else you need to do to be ready?

It is important for coaches to step back and consider if there are any other elements that they need to do to be ready. While this question can only be answered by the coach in specific contexts, we would encourage consideration of operational issues, consideration of the way the coach will prepare themselves for the session, as well as any 'ancillary' support such as bringing in opponents to 'represent' an opposition. Essentially, we suggest that the coach goes through a process of considering the 'what ifs' related to the session.

Step 2: putting the principles into practice

Now the ground work for the session design has been completed, prior to designing the session, the coach needs to develop two resources to simplify the process. As highlighted previously, session design is built on choosing the appropriate learning environment and the appropriate constraints to design-in. Below are the two resources for you to complete for your own coaching.

Design your own environment selector below:

CONSTRAINT-LED SESSION PLANNING: ENVIRONMENT SELECTOR	
NON-PERFORMANCE ENVIRONMENTS	PERFORMANCE ENVIRONMENTS
LEVEL OF REPRESENTATIVENESS OF LEARNING ENVIRONMENT	

Design your own constraint builder below:

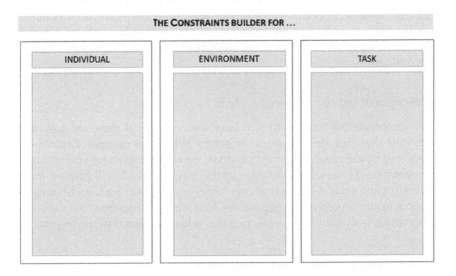

THE **CONSTRAINTS BUILDER FOR …**

| INDIVIDUAL | ENVIRONMENT | TASK |

We also provide these and templates of the tools used in this chapter in the *Resources Section* at the end of the book.

To help coaches frame the session, key features of a CLA session are summarised below. The aim is to provide a 'one-page' resource for coaches that visually brings the key concepts into one place and enables them to connect the key ideas, so they can begin to build the session.

As well as providing key information for each principle, the resource is also interactive as it contains a 'constraints to afford' section, which provides a place for coaches to decide on the constraints they wish to design-in to the session. While all three categories of constraints are considered, coaches should only pick the constraint (or interacting constraints) from the constraint builder that are mapped to the session intentions. Thinking about why and which constraints to choose is assumed as given once the coach 'fills in' this section, but the coach is also asked to consider when she will utilise the constraint. A key message is that manipulating constraints is the mechanism for creating variability and any subsequent (in)stability, therefore, answering this question should be undertaken alongside decisions about how much variability is going to be designed-in to the session. We will cover this shortly.

Step 3: completing the session planner

Below we provide a template that you may wish to use when designing your CLA session. The planner can be understood in terms of four vertical panels and the horizontal 'tasks', which are designed to cover key phases

CONSTRAINT-LED SESSION PLANNING

PURPOSE:

Instead of the traditional skill session where athletes practice their technique, a CLA session is designed to prepare performers for the competition environment with a focus on '*making it real*' session. This approach requires coaches to design-in the affordances that will provide invitations for action. Consider why, which and when to provide the constraints to afford. Additionally, it requires consideration of **repetition without repetition**. This is achieved by adjusting the level of **variability** and **in(stability)** or **chaos** designed into sessions.

CONSTRAINTS TO AFFORD

- You need to identify the affordances that will provide invitations for action.
- Constraints can be designed-in to your practice task to invite these actions.
- Consider why, which and when to provide the constraints.

Task constraint to invite:

1. . . . .
2. . . . .

Individual constraint to invite:

1. . . . .
2. . . . .

Environment constraint to invite:

1. . . . .
2. . . . .

CLA Practice

Representative Practice

-**Purpose & Consequence**

Repetition without Repetition

-**Variability & In(stability)**

COACH ROLE

The key role to get the session design right.

Use the **GROW** questions in your Planning Guide to design the session.

REPRESENTATIVE PRACTICE

- You need to consider how much you want practice to look and feel like the real thing.
- Ask yourself if the tasks will lead to the emergence of intentions, perceptions and actions in your athletes that mirror those seen in the performance environment.

PURPOSE & CONSEQUENCE

- Giving the task a clear purpose and ensuring there are consequences is a key part of ensuring that athletes perform at competition intensity.
- VERY clear measures of success need to be communicated to the athletes.
- Consequences need to matter to the athletes.

REPETITION WITHOUT REPETITION

- The set goal can be doing repetition after repetition or by repetition without repetitions.
- The coach needs to work out how much variability to add into the session.
- Variability can be at an individual, environmental or task level.

VARIABILITY & IN(STABILITY)

- Variability can be changed systematically or randomly.
- At critical values, changing a variable can lead to a change in behaviour (intentions, emotions, perception–action).
- Coaches need to be aware of the implications for placing individuals in these critical (red) zones.

Figure 6.4 An overview of the key aspects of a CLA session.

of the session. A key feature of the design is the introduction of dials to explicitly consider the level of representativeness and variability designed in to the different phases of the session. Essentially, the purpose of the dials is to encourage coaches to manipulate the levels of task representativeness and adaptive variability during different phases of the session by considering the affordances that are designed-in and manipulating constraints. The top panel focuses on the session goals and can be populated from the GROW process undertaken previously. Note that the session goals should link to the level of skill that connects to the 'method' which is effectively an expression of the intentions of the session (i.e. to explore to develop co-ordination, to learn to adapt, or to focus on executing the skill in the performance environment).

The next panel refers to the level of representativeness of the practice task. While the ideas of representative learning design have been misconceived by some who suggest that adopting such ideas means that performers should only ever practise by playing the real game, this is not the case. Adopting the ideas of RLD means that the coach considers the performance environment and decides how much representativeness he or she wants in the practice task. Indeed, as discussed earlier, for very good reasons, he or she may decide that high levels of representativeness are not needed at a specific point in time, particularly when working with beginners. However, creating practice tasks that are low in representativeness does not mean that the key principles of a CLA are ignored and concepts such as perception–action coupling, co-adaptation and self-organisation are still essential requirements. The colouring of the dial to include a red and green zone is designed to emphasise this point with the 'red zone' representing any task where these principles are not considered. For example, a task would be placed in the red zone if performers were required to hit balls off a tee, when the sport requires learning to hit a moving ball. We would add, that learning to couple hitting to hit a *moving* ball is the key principle to underpin RD here and modifying tasks by using different balls and bats or racquets would still be classed as using a representative task, even though it may rate low on the scale. We will illustrate how these dials may be used to 'turn-up' or 'turn-down' the level of representativeness of practice within a session in examples in the practical chapters.

The third panel relates to the constraints that will be utilised in the session. In the constraints section, TIE, refers to task, individual and environmental constraints. Here, the coach simply puts a tick (check mark) alongside the category of constraints that will be used in the session and writes the name of the constraint along the top of the box. The separation into tasks is designed to allow the coach to modify the constraints within the session. Hence, Tasks 2–4, would reflect adding in, removal or manipulations of the designed in constraint. Of course, the session may have fewer or more than four phases; template lesson planners are provided for two, three and four tasks in the *Resources* section. Within each 'constraints' box, the coach

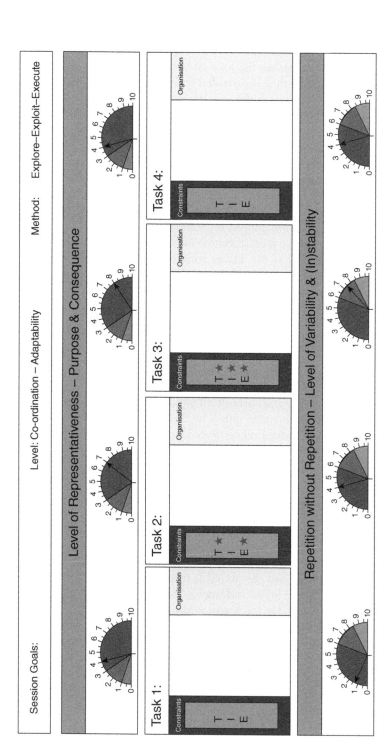

Figure 6.5 The CLA session planner.

could summarise the task or if she has a name for the practice task, simply write the name in here. The organisation section allows the coach to illustrate the layout of the task and any equipment needs.

The final panel considers the level of variability that is to be designed-in to each task. Again, a dial is provided to invite coaches to manipulate the level of variability to match the current ability level of the performer during the session. The zones here are framed to reflect levels of variability that are likely to result in; (i) a strong likelihood of success in the task but wherever possible promote exploration and enhanced dexterity and hence adaptability (i.e. the green zone), (ii) instability that will require the leaner to search for new solutions (amber zone) and (ii) too much variability that will result in total failure (i.e. the red zone). Here, the coach will often need to make 'best guesses' as to which zone a task will be in, but over time and with systematic reflection should be able to become more accurate. When designing-in variability, it is recommended that the initial task sits in the green zone with a shift to the amber zone followed by a shift back into the green zone. This structure would enable the performer to feel confident and successful at the start of the session and leave the session in the same frame of mind (Renshaw et al., 2012).

Step 4: systematic reviews and reflections

Building systematic reviewing and reflection is an essential part of CLA coaching practice. Given that learning is a non-linear process, it is difficult to plan whole programmes in advance as the response of performers to coaching interventions can often be unpredictable, with sudden jumps in performance and indeed regressions being possible. A connected coaching programme is therefore emergent and co-created by the coach and the performers. Below we provide a debriefing resource that coaches can use to formalise this process. A five-step process framed around five questions is provided to learn from every aspect of the design and execution of the CLA practice session. Question 1 frames the reflection in terms of the original goals and expectations and pays specific attention to the affordances that were designed-in to the session. Question 2 invites the coach to reflect on what actually happened and breaks this into three aspects; the design of the session, the coaching and the actual learning that took place. Question 3 drills deeper into these areas and asks what went well and why. Here, the coach is asked to consider the learning design and the impact of what was said, with specific focus on the instructional and informational constraints provided during the session. Questions 4 and 5 focus on the future, with question 4 asking what can be improved and how, before Question 5 invites the coach to consider the most important findings from the reflection process by considering the three tings to continue doing and the three factors to change in future practice.

CLA SESSION DEBRIEF

PURPOSE:
To learn from every aspect of the design and execution of the CLA PRACTICE SESSION.

Q1 WHAT WERE YOU AIMING TO ACHIEVE?

- What goals or expectations did you have for today's activities using the session?
- What affordances were learners invited to act upon?

Q2 WHAT ACTUALLY HAPPENED?

- What were the specific details of **your** performance?
- Design of Session
- Coaching
- Learning

Q3 WHAT WENT WELL AND WHY IN THESE AREAS?
Learning Design: Creating effective learning environments

Learning Design:	What you Said
Constraints to afford	Instructional Constraints
Representative Learning Design	Informational Constraints
Repetition without Repetition	

Q4 IN HINDSIGHT, WHAT CAN BE IMPROVED & HOW?
Learning Design: Creating effective learning environments

Learning Design:	What you Said
• Constraints to afford	Instructional Constraints
• Representative Learning Design	Informational Constraints
• Repetition without Repetition	

Q5 WHAT ARE OUR TOP THREE THINGS TO CONTINUE AND TO CHANGE IN FUTURE PRACTICE SESSIONS?

Three things to continue doing	1. 2. 3.	Three things to continue doing	1. 2. 3.

Figure 6.6 The CLA session de-briefer.

Summary

The last two chapters have focussed on 'bridging the gap' between the theory and practice of CLA with the aim of providing the tools to enable coaches to build their own CLA practice sessions. By following the guidelines provided, we hope that coaches will feel more confident in designing CLA sessions that are tailored to their own contexts and needs. In the final part of the book, we will attempt to bring CLA to life by providing examples of CLA sessions in athletics, invasion games (specifically in hockey) and golf. We will use real-life case studies to model the processes outlined in this chapter. We would point out that each case is not based on any one individual or group we have worked with, but the cases are often an amalgam of ideas.

Part III

A constraints-led approach

Constraints in action

7 A constraints-led approach to coaching field hockey

Introduction

The aim of this chapter is to demonstrate how the constraints-led approach can be applied in the context of international field hockey. Here, we draw on the experiences of Danny Newcombe, a co-author of the book who is applying a CLA in action within domestic and international field hockey contexts. Danny has been the assistant coach for a men's national team for the past seven years. In addition, he has been the head coach of an English National League club for the past three years. First, we take the reader through the step-by-step process employed when designing and adapting practice environments in a field hockey context. Following this, we bring the constraints builder to life by discussing how a range of different constraints pertinent to this context can be employed. Next, we introduce the case study, which begins with an analysis of the current landscape of the national team, followed by implementing the GROW planning process as per Chapter 5. To simplify this section, where appropriate, it will be written from the first-person perspective of Danny. This activity sets the scene for the session design we unpack in the following sections. The session planner section then provides an example of the three linked practices and demonstrates how a coach might systematically design-in affordances to illustrate the application of the constrain to afford principle to the practice design process as well as varying the amount of representativeness and variability designed-in to their practice tasks. Finally, we provide a reflection from the coaching team on the practice environments delivered. The next section brings to life the three-step practice design process employed by Danny and his coaching teams.

Offer key affordances

Step one is to build an environment that provides learners with the opportunity to engage with the affordances related to the development focus (session intention). By using knowledge of the sport, it is the role of the coach to facilitate these opportunities for action through the manipulation of the *task* constraints. For example, if the intention of the session is to facilitate an improvement in a player's ability to defend a large space, in a 1 vs 1 context, versus an opposition player who has the ability to attack at high speed, the environment must be designed to offer the player the opportunity to engage with related affordances. In this example, we would need to adapt the playing space, ensuring it is large enough to facilitate high-speed 1 vs 1 contests. In addition, the start positions of the attacker and defender would need to offer the attacking player a large space to attack. Furthermore, it is important to manage both the orientation and positioning of the players in relation to the goal, to ensure a situation where the defender organises their movement solutions in a representative manner.

Invite and encourage interaction with key affordances

Step 2 involves manipulating the constraints of the practice environment to encourage players to engage with the important affordances in an effective and efficient manner as they self-organise to solve the problem presented. For example, if the intention of the session is to encourage players to pass the ball earlier, it is essential that the practice environment not only provides the learners with opportunities to pass the ball early but also exaggerates (see Renshaw et al., 2015) and thus *invites* those actions. The manipulation of the *task* constraint to provide likely opportunities (but not 100% certain ones) can be achieved through creating numerical superiority by ensuring that the attacking team have at least one more player than the defence in a threatening attacking zone. While a traditional approach to this problem may be to simply create imbalanced teams (i.e. 4 vs 3, 3 vs 2, 2 vs 1), simply giving a team an advantage without requiring them to 'earn it' may lead to team co-ordination solutions that are less representative of the game and lead to a reduction in action fidelity (i.e. it looks like the real thing). Alternative approaches might be to reduce the number of defenders in the immediate area in ways that replicate those that happen in games. For example, in a game an overload might emerge due to a slow recovery run, a defender getting out of position, or perhaps a player being slow back to their feet after a minor injury. Coaches can therefore analyse games to identify the range of possible scenarios and then design them into their practice. For example, the coach could simulate the scenario of a defender being caught out of position after a change of possession by putting a temporal constraint on his or her 'recovery' run to give the attacking team a short time window to exploit their numerical superiority. Alternatively, the coach may require defenders to start in 'poor' positions where a numerical superiority can be exploited, *if* the attackers can attune to the available affordances (i.e. of an out of position defender). Developing representative scenarios such as these will afford the learner the correct context to attune to the available affordances and develop the perception–action couplings needed to pass the ball early more often. This environment manipulation should create a scenario where there is a 'potential' unmarked teammate in a threatening position at the moment that our player receives the ball providing an excellent opportunity for our learners to learn to look and perceive this affordance and pass the ball early. In addition, the introduction of *task* constraints, for example, in the form of a reward-based points system that invites learners to successfully passes the ball early when a 'good' affordance emerges during performance, may result in learners utilising the process of self-organisation to search for functional affordances. This process is a valuable tool in educating the attention of players as they search for opportunities to earn points within the reward structure.

Avoid the over-constraining trap

A key goal of Step 3 is to ensure that the designing-in of constraints does not lead to *over constraining* players and forcing them to make the desired response. While the desired actions are certainly encouraged and, indeed, invited by the coach's design, it is important to re-emphasise that the action should not be forced and should emerge as the learner searches through the dynamically available affordances within the environmental and task constraints. A key point for performers is not just about learning to identify *which* affordance to use but also *when* and then *how* to use it. If the decision to act upon the emergence of an affordance comes from exploration of the landscape of affordance available in the environment rather than being forced by the task constraint to use one affordance, we can be more confident that functional, transferable perception–action synergies will emerge. Typical examples of over-constraining tasks include imposing rules such as, a 'minimum of five passes' prior to scoring or the ubiquitous 'two touches only' rule when in possession. An analogy from an urban design perspective to show how not to over-constrain would be that if an architect wanted to guide walkers around the park she may create a series of connected concrete paths surrounded by lawns to reach the gate on the opposite side of the park. This would invite walkers to walk on different paths, but it does not force them to take one path (or indeed any path as they could still walk on the grass) by giving them no option. Another example of an architect over-constraining the environment would be to force walkers to stay on the path by building high walls alongside it. In terms of judging the success of the design, with regards the desired outcome goal (i.e. they walk on the path *most* of the time; they pass the ball forward and early *most* of the time), then there is compelling evidence that the practice has being constrained in a functional way.

As can be seen from the previous discussion, the ability to learn to choose the most appropriate affordance at any one moment is a key part of learning to play games; however, as we began to highlight above, in their desire to focus practice to achieve one specific goal, there is often a temptation by coaches to *over-constrain* practice by introducing rules or restrictions to explicitly force desired actions (see Partington & Cushion, 2013). As highlighted, a 'two touches only' *task* constraint is a common way that coaches use to force their learners to pass the ball early. By introducing a 'two touches' rule, the coach prescribes intentionality, which, in turn, shapes perception and action (of attackers *and* defenders). In line with the comments above, removing the decision about 'when' to pass from the learner prevents him/her from learning to identify and attune to the key affordances related to 'when' to pass early or when best to hold onto the ball. Two-touch also prescribes the decision of where to stand for defenders, as once the first touch is made, the attacker has solved the problem for the defender. *Over constraining* task constraints stop the natural processes of self-organisation based on the perceived affordances in the environment. For example, at times it might be important to recognise when a pass should be made on the first or second touch and when it might be beneficial to dribble the ball to space or slow play down by keeping possession of the ball. So, the question for coaches is how they can promote effective engagement to achieve set session goals with the environment presented without forcing it.

Apply an understanding of co-adaptation

While not an actual step that Danny goes through in his session design, one key concept of ED he focusses upon when designing a session is that of co-adaptation. Co-adaptation (as we presented in Chapter 3) is the continuous interactions that emerge as athletes co-adapt to each other's behaviours (i.e. team mates and opponents) while self-organising to achieve their goal-directed behaviour. The concept of co-adaptation can therefore be utilised by coaches as a powerful tool to facilitate an implicit behaviour change in the players. Within the performance environment, the opposition team are the provider of an unpredictable dynamic instability that players must self-organise against in order to be successful. This is in contrast to other more static constraints such as pitch dimensions and the goal directed behaviour. As the players co-adapt against this instability, they will be building dexterous perception–action synergies that are truly representative of the performance context. Therefore, a good way to create co-adaptation in a team is for the coach to manipulate the 'opposition' (in practice). In training, the concept is operationalised by:

> Applying task constraints to the defending team to facilitate a behaviour change in the attacking team.
>
> Applying task constraints to the attacking team to facilitate a behaviour change in the defending team.

An example of how to create co-adaptability to meet a session intention

As we mentioned above, the implementation of two-touch play in practice is a common solution for coaches who want their players to move the ball forward quickly. However, as we also highlighted in the previous section, this task constraint over-constrains both attackers and defenders. If the principle of co-adaptation is used to design a session with the intention of facilitating the attacking team to pass the ball early, coaches can use a range of constraints to influence the behaviour of the defending team. For example, rewarding the defending team by having them close down the attackers and increase the pressure on the attacking player in possession of the ball is one solution. Defenders can be encouraged to close down the ball carrier by awarding them points based on how quickly they 'engage' the ball carrier. For example, if the coach counts down from five to one, the number on which they 'engage' the ball carrier is the number of points they are awarded. The winning team is the one who score the most points at the end of the game. An alternative constraint would be to provide the defending team with an opportunity to win an additional defending player for their team if they can consistently put pressure on the ball within a set time frame over a series of possessions. The consequences of placing these task constraints on the defence will be a resultant co-adaptive behaviour by the attacking team. Experiential knowledge shows that the attacking players will adopt self-organising solutions and pass the ball early to make it difficult for the defending team to close the attackers down and negate the opportunity to earn the additional defending player back.

The constraints builder for field hockey

The following section presents the reader with pertinent constraints for consideration in a field hockey context. In Figure 7.1 we present a constraints builder employed for field hockey. The panel comprises three sections, each representing one of the three core constraint categories, namely *individual*, *environment* and *task*.

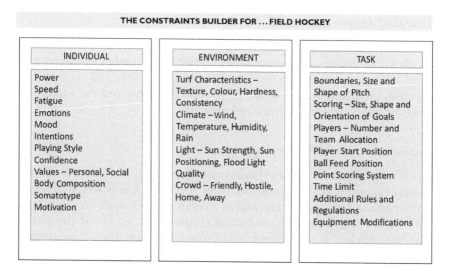

Figure 7.1 The constraint builder for field hockey.

Individual field hockey constraints

While there are a wide range of *individual* constraints for hockey players, perhaps the most important is the intentions of a player that act as the key organising feature shaping cognitions, emotions, perceptions and actions. An example of how a coach can influence a player's intentions, is through the presentation of the *principles of the game*. A player that understands the principles of the game can apply them to the game contexts in which they find themselves in and as a result they act explicitly or implicitly to shape perception–action couplings in specific moments. The recently published GB Hockey, *Talent Development Framework* (https://view.joomag.com/ great-britain-hockey-93026-gbh-talent-development-framework-booklet/ 0794501001518100531?short) provides excellent examples of attacking principles. For example, having an understanding of the guiding attacking principle of *Forward, First, Fast* will encourage players to select and execute the best mode and method to move the ball forward in an attacking context. In a CLA, the instructions given and the questions asked by a coach are more powerful when grounded in the principles of play. For example, 'I am interested in why you thought that was the right time to play forwards?' is a question that could be employed to help manipulate a player's intentions and constrain conscious processes like strategy, in addition to unconscious processes like the perception of, and interaction with, affordances. However, true understanding of the principle must be developed through 'doing' and knowing 'of' the environment. Knowing why *Forward, First, Fast* is a desirable principle can only be realised by experiencing the relative effects of slow build-up play in contrast to a *Forward, Fast, First* intentions. Coaches therefore need to develop an understanding of the principles of play by having players learn them 'in action'.

Task field hockey constraints

The *task* constraints that are most commonly manipulated by hockey coaches are pitch boundaries, goal orientations, the number of players allocated to each team, the starting position of the players and the ball feed position, the manipulation of the point scoring system and the addition of any time limits, additional rules and regulations.

Environmental field hockey constraints

Environmental constraints for hockey are significantly impactful in shaping human behaviour but manipulating them is notably less practical in nature than changing task constraints, and as a result requires more creativity from the coach. A significant environmental constraint in hockey is the surface type with hockey at the highest level being exclusively played on artificial surfaces. However, these surfaces can vary in terms of; base (sand or water based); texture (high or low grip – high friction vs low friction); moisture level (dry or saturated), consistency (even versus variable bounce) and hardness (high or low bounce). All of these different physical environmental constraints act to shape the intentions, perception and actions of the players. For example, if a turf has high bounce characteristics it is advantageous when controlling the ball for players to adapt their movement solutions; normally, this is achieved by positioning the stick in a more vertical position. In international hockey, players are constantly exposed to a wide variety of surfaces to which they must 're-calibrate' actions to adapt very quickly. To that end, coaches should consider systematically varying the training pitches they utilise (or, where possible, make alterations to the turf characteristics) in order to support the emergence of players with adaptable movement solutions (dexterity) to exploit different pitch characteristics.

Field hockey case study

Introduction – the current landscape

As highlighted above, the case study is centred around a performance field hockey context. The team Danny coaches is currently ranked in the top 25 international teams in the world (current FIH world rankings) and takes part in regular international tournaments on a European, Commonwealth and World level. The squad is made up of approximately 30 players, all aged between 17 and 30 years. The majority of the players operate as part-time or semi-professional hockey players, requiring them to balance work, domestic and international hockey commitments. On average, the group has between 50 and 60 contact days per year. The majority of training contact time is 'camp' based, comprising 4 × 2-hour training sessions across two-day periods. Additionally, the team is brought together approximately four days before each tournament. The group is working hard to build on its recent significant improvement with the goal of *continuing to narrow the gap* between the current level of performance and that of the leading teams in the world.

In line with every other top team in the world, the team has access to a performance analysist who records and collects data on each Game. Figure 7.2 provides a stripped-down example of the performance analysis data received by the coaching team following five competitive fixtures played at a recent high-ranking tournament. All five games were played against higher-ranked international teams. The analysis provides the performance outcomes achieved by both teams, including: score; number of circle possessions; number of shots; penalty corners and penalty strokes. As can be observed in the data, a significant point of difference between the team Danny coaches and the higher-ranked teams was the number of open-play shots taken and as a result the number of open play goals scored (i.e. X vs Y). In addition, the analysis provides two ratios, the number of goals scored per shot and the number of goals scored per circle possession. This data reveal the quality of the opportunities created alongside the ability of the team to convert them. The 'GOT' (Goal Opportunity Threat) score provides an indication of the quantity and quality of the shooting opportunities created. Each shooting opportunity is given a score out of 5. For example, unopposed shots in the centre of the attacking circle are valued as being the most desirable opportunities and are awarded 5 points. Shooting opportunities are awarded fewer points as the shooting angle decreases and scoring becomes more difficult, for example shots from close to the goal line are awarded 1 point. In addition, if any shot is judged to be contested by a defender the score is reduced by −1. Finally, the 'Team Shot Corner Stroke Ratio' (TSCSR) score provides a percentage likelihood of winning the game based on the scoring opportunities generated by both teams (the shots at goal/the number of corners/ penalty strokes earnt). Previous data shows that any score of over 0.40 provides an excellent opportunity to win the game. As can be viewed from Figure 7.2, the team's average 'TSCSR' score for the tournament was 0.33, clearly identifying an area for performance improvement.

Based on the analysis of the data and conversations with the coaching and playing group, the key rate limiter was determined as the lack of ability to create goal-scoring opportunities from open play (12 open play shots to the oppositions 36), particularly when playing against higher ranked teams. As confirmed by the post-match analysis, shooting opportunities were only one-third of those created by our opponents and when they did emerge, were quickly prevented due to highly organised, tight defending. Deeper analysis looking at our attacks after we had re-gained possession in open play in their own half, demonstrated that the players were turning down the opportunity to counter-attack by taking too long to move the ball into the final third. Essentially, the team were failing to follow the principle of *Forward, Fast, First*, as discussed above. Consequently, this was giving opposing defences time to funnel back into organised defensive positions. A team's defence is most disorganised when it loses the ball, particularly when the ball and team are committed to attack and are deep in the opposition half. Consequently, losing the ball at this point, means they are vulnerable to a fast counter-attack. A counter-attack opportunity is defined by a loss of possession by the opposition team, which could be anywhere on the field, that in-turn facilitates an attacking opportunity against a disorganised defence. Often, this transition of possession facilitates a numerical overload for the attacking team, with the opportunity to exploit a large space defended by fewer defenders (i.e. a large playing area to defender ratio) in the attacking phase and is the reason that a counter-attack offers an excellent opportunity score. An effective counter-attack is therefore characterised by a fast transition from defence to attack where the ball is moved down the field as quickly as possible to exploit out of position defenders and the potential numerical superiority. The counter-attacking opportunity requires exploiting a short temporal window of opportunity and therefore requires playing at high speed, a particularly challenging task constraint as it requires highly precise execution of passes from the attacking team.

Match	Result	Goals For	Goals Against	Attacking Circle Possessions	Opp ACE Poss Total	Open Play Shots	Opp Open Play Shots	PCA Total	Opp PCA Total
1	D	1	1	11	10	4	5	0	2
2	L	0	3	17	13	3	5	3	2
3	L	3	4	6	18	1	8	3	7
4	L	2	3	13	20	3	11	2	4
5	W	3	2	17	18	1	7	5	1
TOTALS		9	13	64	79	12	36	13	16

Match	Open Play Goals	Opp Open Play Goals	PCA Goals	Opp PCA Goals	Penalty	Opp Penalty	Open Play Goals Per Shots	Open Play Goals Against
1	1	0	0	1	0	0	0.25	0.00
2	0	1	0	1	0	1	0.00	0.20
3	0	1	3	3	0	0	0.00	0.13
4	1	2	1	1	0	0	0.33	0.18
5	0	2	3	0	0	0	0.00	0.29
TOTALS	2	6	7	6	0	1	0.12	0.16

Match	PCA Conv Rate	Opp PCA Conv Rate	Goals Per Circle	Goals Against Per Circe Possession	TSCSR	Opp TSCSR	GOT Score	Opp GOT Score
1	0.00	0.50	0.09	0.10	0.36	0.64	12	21
2	0.00	0.50	0.00	0.23	0.43	0.57	22	26
3	1.00	0.43	0.50	0.22	0.21	0.79	19	56
4	0.50	0.25	0.15	0.15	0.25	0.75	20	57
5	0.60	0.00	0.18	0.11	0.43	0.57	29	27
TOTALS	0.42	0.34	0.18	0.16	0.33	0.66	20.4	37.4

Figure 7.2 Performance analysis data from five international field hockey fixtures. The data includes (both for and against): Goals, Attacking Circle Possessions (ACE), Open Play Shots, Penalty Corner Attack (PCA), Open Play Goals, Penalty Corner Attack Goals (PCA), Penalty, Open Play Goals Per Shot, Penalty Corner Attack Conversion Rate (PCA Conv Rate), Goals Per Circle Possession, Team Shot Corner Stroke Ratio (TSCSR), Goal Opportunity Threat Score (GOT).

Based on the background and analysis above, the coaching team decided that one of the most effective ways to increase the scoring opportunities was to place a focus on improving the team's ability to counter-attack. Discussions with the players revealed that a significant barrier to using a counter-attacking strategy was one of perception, with the players either not aware of when to counter-attack or turning down emergent counter-attack opportunities. It was clear from the exploratory conversations with the players that maintaining possession was valued higher than the opportunity to counter-attack and the associated increase risk of losing possession. This mindset was particularly evident when playing against higher-ranked teams and, as a result, it was clear that the players did not know how to manage risk-reward, that is, when to play carefully and make safer slower passes or when to play faster, making higher risk passes where loss of possession is a greater risk. We address the constraint of player intentions in the case study we present later in the chapter.

Traditional counter-attack practices

Practice at counter-attacking has traditionally been very prescribed with players told where to run and when and how to pass. A good example of such practice is the typical three-man weave seen in basketball. This unopposed practice rehearses what is perceived to be the ideal solution. However, due to the dynamic nature of invasion games, we would argue that an ideal solution does not exist as the solution required is never the same for two different counter-attack opportunities. The aim of any counter-attack practice is therefore the development of players who can effectively react to the emergent dynamic environment, co-adapting their intra and inter-personal co-ordination patterns to optimise emergent counter-attack opportunities. Therefore, the practice environments provided must facilitate the construction of these effective and adaptable behaviours. The following case study provides a worked example of how Danny attempted to facilitate these behaviours in practice.

GROW planning process

A completed example of the four-step GROW planning process (Figure 7.3) and the additional elements of the design process (GROW) are unpacked in the following sections.

What is the goal/intention for this session?

The goal of the session was to improve the team's ability to exploit and execute counter-attack opportunities.

G GOAL	R REALITY	O OPTION	W WAY FORWARD
What's the goal/ intention for this session? Improve consistency in execution of counter attack opportunities. **How does this link to the overall goal?** Increase the number of open play shots (goals). **The focus for learning is . . .** Consistency of execution, both in possession or as a supporting team member. Develop understanding of which side and when relative width in attack is required.	**What's the current skill level?** Adaptability **What affordances of the performance environment do you want to design-in to practice?** ○ Transition in possession ○ Defensive disorganisation ○ Width & depth ○ Attacking overload ○ Fast defensive re-organisation	**Where on the ENVIRONMENT DESIGN CONTINUUM will you place the session?** Highly representative **Which PRACTICE ENVIRONMENTS will you use?** Small Unit Play, Small-Sided Game, Macro Game **What CONSTRAINTS from the ENVIRONMENT DESIGN BUILDER will you use and how will you manipulate them?** ○ Player intentions, pitch boundaries, players and allocation, ball feed manipulation, point scoring system **How will you measure performance?** ○ % of counter attack opportunities executed successfully **We will know we have been successful if:** ○ **We can see** . . . Clean, fast, flowing counter attacks ○ **The data shows** . . . An increase in open play shots and goals ○ **The coach says** . . . Provides support for the defensive team ○ **The athlete feels** . . . Like it is too easy to score	**How do you prepare the environment?** The coaching team need to remain relaxed and reward the correct intent from players. **How do you prepare the athlete(s)?** Emphasise the need to be relaxed but ruthless. Set the challenge but empathise that it is not an easy task to avoid player frustration. **Anything else to be ready?** Performance analyst ready to film footage and perform statistical analysis.

Figure 7.3 GROW analysis in preparation for counter-attack development session.

How does this link to the overall goal?

Improving the ability to counter-attack will increase the number of goal attempts in open play particularly when playing against higher ranked teams.

The focus for learning is?

Three linked areas were identified as the significant 'rate limiters' to counter-attack performance and formed the focus for learning. The first problem identified was a poor level of recognition by the player in possession of when and where to play forwards; this results in the counter-attack opportunities disappearing before they could be exploited. The second problem was an inability to adapt to the player on the ball, with supporting team members struggling to identify when and where to position themselves in the field of play to support the attack. This results in players collapsing the playing space and making it easier to defend against. The final problem: once a support player received the ball there was a lack of accuracy in the technical execution, with players commonly making ball-handling errors, for example, the poor execution of passes when moving at pace.

What's the current skill level?

The current skill level of the group was identified as being mixed, with some players at the level of 'coordination' and others at 'adaptability'.

What affordances of the performance environment do you want to design-in to the practice?

The aim of the training session is to develop the team's ability to exploit and execute counter-attack opportunities, therefore, the practice needs to provide the players with multiple opportunities to practise counter-attacking. The practice environments provided need to include an opportunity generated from a transition in possession to exploit defensive dis-organisation along with the potential for an attacking overload in a large space in attack. Additionally, the amount of time allowed to successfully execute the attack needs to be short due to a rapidly re-organising defence.

Which practice environment will you use?

Using the environment selector Danny utilises within his invasion game of field hockey (Figure 7.4), the coaches decided to employ pitch-orientated, performance environments that are more representative of the performance environment.

ENVIRONMENT SELECTOR FOR . . . FIELD HOCKEY

UNOPPOSED PRACTICES				MACRO GAME – 8–11 pps
	OPPOSED PRACTICES 1–2 pps		SMALL-SIDED GAME – 4–7 pps	
	BACKYARD GAMES 1v0, 1 with 1		SMALL-UNIT PLAY – 2–4 pps	
BACKYARD PRACTICE				

NON-DIRECTIONAL   DIRECTIONAL   MULTI-DIRECTIONAL   DIRECTIONAL

NON PITCH-ORIENTATED   PITCH-ORIENTATED   NON PITCH-ORIENTATED   PITCH-ORIENTATED

NON-PERFORMANCE ENVIRONMENTS   **PERFORMANCE ENVIRONMENTS**

◄──────── **LEVEL OF REPRESENTATIVENESS OF LEARNING ENVIRONMENT** ────────►

Figure 7.4 The environment selector – field hockey example.

Which practice environments will you use?

Three practices were selected by the coaching team to bridge the learning gap. Namely, a small-unit practice, a small-sided game and a macro game. These specific practices are presented in the session planner section that follows.

Which constraints from the environment builder will you use and how will you manipulate them?

The constraint builder (Figure 7.1) was employed to help the coaches select the constraints to manipulate in the design and adaptation of the practice environments. These involved a combination of task and individual constraints. The task constraints included adaptations of size and shape of the playing area (boundaries), the point-scoring system employed, the number and allocation of players on each team and an introduction of time limits. The coaches influenced the players' intentions and playing style within the practice environments; these manipulations fall under the category of individual constraints.

We will know we have been successful if . . .

We see an improvement in the consistency of our counter-attack execution in competitive fixtures. The counter-attacks will be precise, fast and flowing. Supporting players will move themselves into advantageous positions in the field of play and we will be able to observe the teamwork as a unit, effectively adapting individual movements as they co-adapt with each other. We will see the players spending a minimal amount of time in possession of the ball and making accurate decisions regarding where it will be most advantageous to play forwards. This will facilitate the efficient movement of the ball into the attacking circle. The players will begin to feel like it is too easy as they consistently execute a series of connected actions.

Earlier in the chapter, we provided examples of how a field hockey coach can design practice environments to improve performance. In the following section we will illustrate how a CLA session can be brought to life by using the session planner process we introduced in the last chapter. The aim of this element of the case study is to exemplify how coaches can employ a range of different practice environments to bridge the learning gap.

The session planner – explore, exploit, execute

Overview: the session plan below (Figure 7.5) presents the three practice tasks that were designed to bridge the learning gap. As indicated on the RLD and variability dials, the levels of representativeness and variability that were designed-in is increased across the three practice tasks. Task 1 is designed to allow the players to 'tune' in to the practice landscape and facilitate the *exploration* of new solutions to the problem. Task 2 is designed to

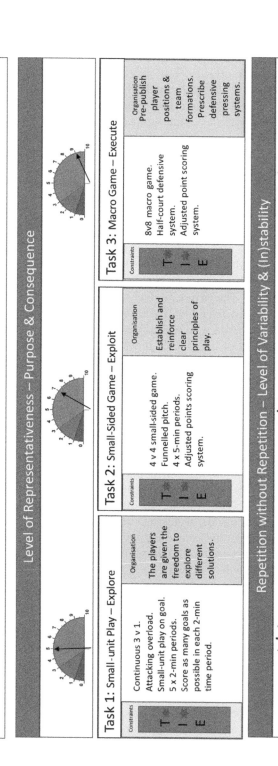

Figure 7.5 CLA session plan – field hockey (counter-attack).

develop the players ability to *exploit* the affordances presented within the practice task. The focus of Task 3 is to develop the players ability to *execute* counter-attack opportunities under pressure.

Task 1: a small-unit practice. The players will be required to complete 5 × 2-minute blocks of a 3 vs 1 small-unit play. The task is designed to provide the players with the necessary time and space to *explore* different movement solutions within a counter-attacking context. The *task* constraint manipulation (attacking overload) will provide a moderate level of representativeness (3). This is a deliberate policy to facilitate the likelihood of a greater initial level of success for the attacking team (see Chapter 5). We want the players to have significant numbers of ball contacts (technical executions such as passing and receiving without losing momentum) while still maintaining relevant affordances from the performance environment (i.e. directional and a defender). The 2-minute time limit is included in Task 1 to encourage the players to complete the task at pace to ensure that the movement solutions were representative and a functional fit with the performance environment.

Task 2: a small-sided game. Figure 7.6 shows the 4 vs 4 small-sided counter-attacking game. The picture on the left depicts the goal that the counter-attacking team (Red) are defending. Here, the pitch boundaries are narrowed towards the goal to create a funnel effect to reduce the playing space to increase the likelihood of a tackle or interception and a transition in possession. On the right, the picture shows the attacking goal and represents the counter-attack phase of play following the transition of possession to the Red team. The pitch boundaries at this end of the field are opened up, which provided players from the Red team with a large space to attack. The players will be required to play 4 × 5-minute blocks of the 4 vs 4 small-sided game. The levels of representativeness and variability designed-in to this task were elevated from Task 1 (7). A manipulation (increase) in the player numbers and the allocation of players to an even-load game (the same number of players on both teams) is predicted to facilitate an increased level of representation (7). To invite the attacking players to move the ball quickly and efficiently into the attacking circle, the point-scoring system will be adapted to encourage the defending players to re-organise quickly in an attempt to dissolve the counter-attack opportunity.

Task 3: the session will finish with 4 × 6-minute blocks of an 8 vs 8 game. In contrast to the previous practice tasks, this task is designed to provide a more limited number of counter-attack opportunities. The motivation behind this practice is to place greater value on each counter-attack opportunity with the aim of replicating the value they have in the performance environment. A further increase in the level of representativeness (9) and variability (8) has been designed-in to this practice task by manipulating a series of *task* constraints. Specifically, this involved an increase in the number of players allocated to each team and a point-scoring system that places a greater value on executing counter-attacks. Furthermore, the defending systems of both teams are to be manipulated to encourage a live transition

Figure 7.6 Counter-attack practice.

of possession in areas of the pitch conducive to counter-attacking (defending deeper in the pitch to invite the opposition team to attack the circle). The scoring system is manipulated to provide additional reward for goals scored via a counter-attack (double points). In addition, an escalating point scoring system over the 4×6-min blocks (i.e. a goal in block 1 earns a team 1 point, a goal in block 2 earns a team 2 points, etc.) will be employed.

Session reflection

This section is written from Danny's point of view: Task 1 is a practice we often use to facilitate the players to 'tune in' to the environment while gaining opportunity for repetition without repetition of the decisions and actions required in a counter-attack context. The execution error rate from the player(s) in possession of the ball at the start of this practice was very high, with the players becoming increasing frustrated with the performance, particularly as they perceived this to be an easy practice. The players adapted and self-organised by slowing the pace of their counter-attacks down. While this facilitated more success, it was clear that the speed at which the players completed the counter-attacks would not be effective in the performance environment and therefore lacked sufficient representativeness. The coaching team spoke to the playing group half way through the practice in an attempt to influence their intentions and increase the speed at which they were counter-attacking. However, upon reflection, the introduction of a points system that rewarded the execution of faster, more efficient counter-attacks would have perhaps been a more impactful solution.

The coaching and playing group all felt that Task 2 created a realism (representativeness) that was missing in Task 1. This was evidenced by the players making similar decisions and evidencing similar actions to those observed in the performance environment. The more natural (and random) facilitation of counter-attacks appeared to help facilitate this improvement in action fidelity. In this task, a lack of understanding of where and when to position themselves was the clear 'rate limiter' to the successful execution of counter-attack opportunities. This was illustrated by the players consistently collapsing space, and as a consequence negating the attacking numerical advantage. A discussion with the players demonstrated that they understood the principle of providing 'stretch' (making the playing space as large as possible), but some players were still struggling to transfer this understanding onto the field of play (see the discussion about understanding the principle of play earlier in the chapter: they 'knew about' but not 'of' the performance environment – and see Chapter 4). Moving forwards, we will add additional task constraints in the form of line markings to the playing area, providing spatial markers that have the potential to guide player positioning. This reflection highlights the challenge coaches face when attempting to transfer 'knowledge about' into 'knowledge of' the environment.

Interestingly, in Task 3 the elevated value of goals in the final block (4 points for a goal or 8 points for a counter-attack goal) facilitated very few counter-attack opportunities. From observing the players behaviour and discussing the practice with them, this was a product of the team in possession of the ball taking significantly less risk in attack for fear of being counter-attacked against. Although this presented less opportunity to practise our counter-attacking it did create the value placed on them and was *representative* of the performance environment. It was interesting to watch the co-adaptation process happening as the teams started to adapt their defending to generate the opportunity to counter-attack. Moving forwards, it will be interesting to observe the impact of a declining point scoring system on player behaviour.

We have seen a positive impact of our sessions on our counter-attack execution in the performance environment and these observations were consistent with the GROW analysis completed prior to the session. The biggest impact has been the improved positioning of our support players, which has significantly improved, evidencing an ability to co-adapt by moving themselves into more advantageous positions. However, we are still demonstrating inconsistency in our ability to execute, with passes still not being delivered to their intended target at crucial moments. We are looking forward to putting our counter-attacking into action against the leading teams in the world over the next 12 months.

Summary

In this chapter we explored the application of the CLA to an international field hockey context. The GROW analysis emphasised the importance of counter-attacking in this context. We highlighted the importance of the constrain to afford principle has on facilitating targeted and transferable development. In addition, we discussed the role different linked practice environments can play in bridging the learning gap. Within these practice tasks we exemplified how different levels of representativeness and variability can be designed-in to the practice. We have provided brief examples of how a CLA could enhance the practice of field hockey coaches. We will build on these ideas in more detail in a forthcoming book in the series: *A Constraint-Led Approach to Field Hockey Coaching*. This book will be jointly written by ourselves and international hockey coaches who will provide the unique examples from their own work with performance and development field hockey players. We look forward to sharing and discussing further ideas with you there.

8 A constraints-led approach to coaching golf

Introduction

Although successful golf performance is predicated on effective course management, where golfers 'navigate' their way around the contours and 'natural and man-made' hazards of each unique hole, much of golf coaching takes place off the course on driving ranges and practice grounds. Clearly, little importance is attached to the environment in terms of its role in shaping the skills needed to play golf and much coaching is focused on developing good golf swings. This separation of the individual and the environment when considering skill learning is common across many sports and has been criticised by those who view the individual and the environment as inseparable when designing skill learning activities. This idea is captured in a relatively new definition of skill (as successful adaptation) proposed by Araújo and Davids (2011a), discussed in the earlier theoretical chapters. This contemporary view, which we use in a CLA, emphasises the importance of learners attuning or adapting to the performance environment as discussed in Chapter 3. The best players are the ones who are best 'adapted' to the environment. This means that learning needs to occur on the course or for the aspiring tour player on as many courses as possible. An additional challenge for these players is that the courses they learn to play on need to help them develop the wide range of capacities (mental, emotional, perceptual and physical) needed to succeed on championship courses. For example, a golfer brought up on the links courses of Scotland, is likely to develop a style of play that is perfectly adapted to these unique playing environments. Hence, successful links golfers are perfectly attuned to the contours of the course, adapt shots to exploit the wind, are expert at bump and run shots, are able to play effective shots from deep rough and get out of deep, deep pot bunkers with steep walls. In contrast, a golfer brought up to play on courses in America, is more likely to be able to hit long and use high-flighted irons to land the ball softly on receptive greens. Top players, who travel around the world, therefore need the adaptive skill sets to excel on all types of courses, in all types of conditions. The average club player who only plays on his/her home course would 'simply' need to become attuned to the one course. Golf coaches should take these contexts into account when working with learners.

The environment shapes the golfer

These brief examples highlight why it is essential to consider the performance environment when working with players. However, for the golf coach, this obligation presents some interesting challenges. For example, when much coaching takes place on artificial surfaces at the driving range, there is a need to find ways of making the environment more representative of the 'real thing'. For example, the hard mat can be very forgiving when a player hits the ground before the ball, allowing the club to 'bounce' and enable a good contact with the ball. However, a similar shot on turf on the course would lead to a very poor contact and outcome. Learning to play by hitting off artificial mats results in players developing a golf swing that is suited to that specific surface. However, attuning to these environments may not transfer to hitting off turf. Spending most of the time hitting off mats may give a golfer a false impression of how well they are hitting the ball and ultimately lead to frustration when they play on the course. Consequently, it would be advantageous if the player could experience the consequences of swing 'errors' when practising at the driving range and even better if practice could be on a more realistic surface. When winter practice precludes the use of turf, adopting a CLA may be helpful. Essentially, the surface needs

Figure 8.1 Hitting off a towel can be used to simulate hitting out of the rough or if used on the driving range to accentuate the importance of making contact with the back of the ball.

to be modified as much as possible to make it more representative of turf so when any contact that is not clean on the ball (i.e. hitting the ground before the ball), the consequences should be a similar outcome as if playing on grass. A simple solution would be to place a towel on the floor and hit the ball off that. If the player hits a full iron shot off the ground (towel) before the ball, this would result in the towel crumpling up and a poor contact with the ball. The same solution can be applied to practising hitting from the rough on the course, when hitting the grass behind the ball can reduce the quality of ball contact.

Knowing the individual

Of course, when taking a position that the individual and environment relationship plays a complementary role in skill learning, equal emphasis should be placed on both but efforts to gain a deep knowledge of the individual should not be reduced as a consequence. When implementing a CLA approach, the first interaction between a coach and player should therefore be a fact-finding mission to uncover as much information as possible. Essential to this process is investigating the background of the individual to understand the context of the player's current golf game; we need to know where he or she has come from and where he or she wants to go in terms of performance.

The history of individuals is crucial and includes finding out more about their work, sporting background, taking account of other sports played, and, importantly, their physical status such as any prevailing conditions, disorders and injuries. The importance to the coach of thorough background knowledge is paramount, prior to even watching a learner play. A brief story about one of the co-authors of the forthcoming CLA golf book in this series, Peter Arnott, a professional golf coach, illustrates this point perfectly. Early in his golfing career, Pete used to work as a surveyor, travelling 300 miles per day. Therefore, when he went to the driving range after work, he was often very stiff in the back, from the hours spent in the car. This stiffness affected his mobility and, ultimately, his golf swing, and at the beginning of his practice session resulted in the low point of his swing being near to his back foot. He, therefore, needed to place the ball further back in his stance to ensure the ball was matched to this low point. As he warmed up and his mobility returned, the low point of the swing moved further forward, and he was able to put the ball further forward in his stance. So, consider a coach who did not know Pete's background looking at his swing and coming to conclusions about why he was hitting the ball fat when the ball was placed in a conventional position in the set-up.

This story highlights the importance of coaches seeing the golf swing as being part of a dynamic system, where a 'one size fits all' approach can negatively impact the golfer's performance. If the coach followed the guidelines in the coaching manual, that is, to place the ball at specific points in the stance for different clubs, the ball might be placed inappropriately and lead to poor ball contact, despite the fact the learner might have made a good swing. For example, in the case of Pete, requiring him to use his three iron with the ball placed just inside his front foot (e.g. as recommended by the coaching books), would risk him hitting the ground behind the ball. Coaches can use a CLA to help players 'find' their low point. If hitting on turf, the coach can use an alignment stick to create a depression in the turf. She then places the ball on the front edge of the depression and asks the player to hit the ball. The place where contact was made with the ground (i.e. where the divot was created) tells the player and coach the low point of the swing. Rather than making a decision based on one ball, the coach should ask her to hit four to five balls to assess the consistency of the low point. Once consistency is confirmed, the golfer should adopt a process of repeat and correct; if the divot is consistently taken before the ball, the player should move his/her stance further forward by the distance behind the ball. If taken in front of the ball, the stance should be moved back. To summarise, the position of the ball in the stance should be seen as dynamic rather than fixed, and players should be encouraged to explore the ball position in his stance at the beginning of every practice session. Additionally, during competition, the ball position in the stance should be viewed as being dynamic and should vary depending on the conditions. For example, not every seven-iron would have the same ball position as it would depend on environmental factors such as slope, type of grass and ground conditions, as well as intentions such as intended trajectory due to wind conditions or the height needed to exploit the pin position/ground conditions. In summary, ball position is dynamic and part of the process of finding a solution to a unique performance problem on every shot. The dynamic nature of practice, required to enhance performance, is aligned with Bernstein's (1967) conceptualisation of practice as 'repetition without repetition', as noted in the theoretical chapters.

It should be clear from the previous discussion that the pursuit of a textbook 'perfect' golf swing with players by coaches is inappropriate and coaching should be tailored to the characteristics of each individual. Going back to our main point in this section, knowing as much as possible about a player's background allows the coach to understand why they swing a golf club in the way they do and informs the way that he/she should talk to the player and inform the learning activities they create. For example, previous sports played will influence the way an individual swings a golf club, with some sports helping (e.g. a rotary swing in hockey) or hindering (e.g. a more linear swing in cricket batting) when a beginner starts to play golf. Knowing the sporting background of a new golfer enables the coach to avoid golf 'jargon' and communicate in a language that he or she understands. For example, if the coach was working with an ex-tennis player and trying to articulate what the swing path for hitting a draw shot is like, (s)he might ask him/her to describe the shape and feel when hitting a topspin drive; a similar action as required in a draw shot. Alternatively, if the client played football, (s)he might ask him/her to imagine the feeling of bending a free kick around the wall into the top corner. Knowing the client's physical history (i.e. fitness level and any previous injuries) also provides more knowledge to understand the 'rate limiters' on the emergent swing of the golfer. For example, knee injuries or lower back pain, can impact the emergent golf swing and should be taken into consideration by the coach.

Once a golfer becomes experienced, he or she will develop a signature golf swing. For example, there may be a 'natural' right to left (a draw or hook), or left to right (a fade or slice) flight trajectory. However, often players can become frustrated with the limitations of their swings and seek to change things through consultation with a coach. Decisions to change established techniques should be carefully considered, as deeply engrained movement patterns are difficult to change. Such decisions are likely to result in a period of instability and accompanying reduction in performance as the player seeks to re-organise. A recent conversation with, Jessica, a nine-handicap golfer, illustrates this point. Jessica had just come back from a lesson with her club pro as her natural shot was to 'slice' her drives as she believed this was the key reason why she could not get her handicap any lower. The coach worked hard with Jessica focussing on the swing mechanics (i.e. the path of the arms) to create a swing path to draw the ball (i.e. move it from right to left in the flight). She had some success on the driving range while repeating the same shot over and over again. Later that afternoon she took her 'new' swing out onto the course with a sense of confidence; she had cracked this! However, to her surprise and frustration, the new swing was not effective, and, in fact, was so deleterious to her scoring she abandoned it after five holes.

Golf coaching and skill learning principles

This example highlights a number of issues related to skill learning in golf. The first question to ask is: was attempting to create a new swing path the right option? One problem was that the coach took this decision without getting detailed information about the player's movement history and without seeing her play on the course. Given she was playing off a handicap of nine, how bad was the 'slice'? Was her performance significantly worse than other low handicap golfers or was she losing shots in other areas of her play? A second factor that may not have helped Jessica was the creation of an internal focus of attention. Requiring the golfer to focus internally can lead to attempts to consciously control movements, which has been shown to lead to slower learning (Gray, 2018). The third issue was the focus on blocked practice (i.e. repetition after repetition of the same shot), which results in better performance in the learning phase, but actually leads to worse performance when transferred to the competitive environment. Research shows that blocked practice leads to an illusion of competence as seen with Jessica (Simon & Bjork, 2001).

Constraints in shaping a shot

An alternative approach adopting CLA principles, would be to create a task where the learner used variable practice alongside an external focus of attention. For example, Jessica could be given a target to hit and asked to explore hitting that target by using different movement solutions. By asking her to hit the target by creating different flight characteristics, such as shaping the ball left-to-right, straight and right-to-left, Jessica would be directed to explore the flight characteristics and through questioning encouraged to link outcomes with how specific movements felt. Task constraints can also be constructed to help players learn to create different flight characteristics. One useful constraint is to create a 'gate' approximately 2 m wide and placed about 3 m in front of the golfer, using two alignment rods (or even two narrow garden canes). The golfer is asked to hit the ball through the gate to hit the target. Figure 8.2 shows the set-up on a course. In this case, the positioning of the gate meant that the golfer had to create draw on the ball to hit the target. In Figure 8.2, Jessica could add in another gate, to the right as we look at the picture. Alternatively, one pole could be placed directly in line with the flag stick and she would be asked to hit to the right and left of the pole in turn.

Figure 8.2 Bend it like Beckham. In the above figure, asking the golfer to hit the ball through the gate in order to hit the target led to the emergence of a golf swing that created 'draw' (right to left swerve) on ball flight.

Of course, the golfer is not allowed to use these poles on the course, so a progression from this practice task would be for learners to use natural features of the course that help them to solve the performance problem by shaping different shots. For example, in Figure 8.2, the golfer could be required to play from behind the trees on either side of the fairway and given the challenge of hitting the flag. Practising on the course is, therefore, the ideal scenario and the golf coach should take every opportunity to take learners out onto the course for more specific transfer. In the discussion above, we have provided a few examples of how the golf coach can design-in constraints into practice to help golfers improve performance. In the following case study, we will illustrate how a constraint-based practice session can be brought to life by using the CLA session planner process we introduced in the last chapter.

A case study: Thomas can't pitch

Introduction

Five years ago, 17-year-old Thomas was introduced to golf by his dad and was instantly hooked. He joined his dad's golf club and played every day over the summer. As an athletic person with good hand–eye co-ordination, Thomas seemed to be something of a natural golfer and within a few years he was playing off an 18 handicap. Fast forward to now and Thomas was a two-handicapper on the fringes of his national squad! To progress, this year Thomas had joined a championship golf course and was enjoying the harder challenge it was presenting. However, despite his hard work, over the last year Thomas had not managed to reduce his handicap at all. Thomas liked to record performance 'stats' and kept a record of his rounds, storing information on a stats package online. The data were particularly revealing. They highlighted that, although he could drive 280 m, he was, in comparison to the pros, attempting too many drives that were unplayable, either out of bounds or not giving himself a clear line of sight to the hole for his second shot (i.e. behind a tree or in thick rough). Most of the bad shots were hooks that put him in trouble. One other weakness Thomas noticed was that his pitching (from 10–50 yards from the pin) was nowhere near the level it needed to be, with the stats package highlighting that his current handicap, when relating to other skill levels, was more like a 12-handicapper than a two-handicapper in this area. Consequently, at the end of the season, Thomas and his dad sat down and reflected on his progress. He had achieved some success winning a few club competitions before his handicap dropped, but now he seemed to have hit a bit of a plateau. With winter coming up he decided he had a perfect opportunity to take stock and 'go back to basics' with the goal of starting next season a better player and in good shape to achieve his next goal. Next season he wanted to get down to scratch or below and play for his national team in competitions. As part of his winter plan, Thomas and his dad decided that he needed to take a series of lessons with a club pro and found out that the club had a number of coaches. Thomas asked around, and while the view was that all the coaches were great, the new guy, Paul, was a little different to the others as he spent less time trying to make fundamental changes to the golf swing and focused more about how to play the golf course. Apparently, Paul's motto was 'improve your score, not your golf swing' and much of his coaching took place on the course, whereas the others spent much of their time coaching on the driving range. From his experiences in other sports, Thomas knew that over-thinking and becoming too technical would not work for him. It seemed Paul was the coach for him and he eagerly booked in for a series of coaching sessions.

The first session: taking stock

Thomas met Paul for his first session in the club café and spent the first half hour answering a wide range of questions about himself and his game. Paul explained that to design an effective coaching programme, best suited to Thomas' needs, he needed to know as much about him as he could. Questions ranged from: what he did for work, his history of movement, any injuries, conditions and disorders that he had, his sporting background and, finally, his thoughts about his own game and how golf should be played. Paul listened to everything Thomas said and was particularly intrigued by the change in Thomas' pitching ability and probed away at this issue. Thomas revealed his frustration to Paul and indicated that he could not understand why he struggled with distance control and strike. Given his length off the tee and his ability to then hit into the green with low irons, he felt he was costing himself needless shots when he was so close to the pin. 'This is ridiculous' was the key phrase that Paul heard him say and could see the anguish and confusion in Thomas' voice and facial expressions. From his experience, Paul felt he might know the answer to the conundrum but wanted to confirm his diagnosis for himself. He took Thomas onto the practice hole and threw eight balls down in various lies and places around the fringe of the green and asked Thomas to chip each ball as close to the pin as possible. The results were mixed with very few of the balls coming to rest near the pin, with some long off the putting surface. Five of the balls were cleanly hit, with a low trajectory that landed firmly at the front of the green and rolled out past the flag. Three of balls were poorly struck. Thomas had hit the ground before the ball with a large divot or as Thomas described 'I hit them fat'. These balls came to rest well short of the flag. The results confirmed to Paul what he had suspected. The problem with Thomas' pitching technique, was that he de-lofted the golf club at impact and had too much shaft lean towards the target at ball address and then at impact, with the ball position predominantly nearer Thomas's trail foot at set-up. This all led to a steeper angle of attack and resulted in lower ball flight with little to no spin on the golf ball. Paul sat Thomas down and asked if he could explain his results. After watching Thomas initially struggling to explain it, Paul directed him towards thinking about the 'effect of his action' rather than the action itself. Paul used the analogy of an aircraft crash-landing onto the ball rather than a smooth landing on a runway. Paul then moved the conversation to how Thomas might go about changing the 'effect' of his action in such a way that would improve the mechanics of his technique. Thomas came up with several suggestions regarding what he might do to improve his pitching action. Rather than confirm whether the changes would work or not, Paul smiled at Thomas and said, 'let's go to the short game area and find out if this works'. Paul wanted to afford Thomas with the opportunity to explore, discover and self-organise a movement pattern rather than prescribe a fix.

Paul placed lots of balls round the short game area, but before asking him to hit any of them, Paul now introduced Thomas to athlete's foot powder and sprayed the face of Thomas's wedge with it. Paul explained that when the clubface made contact with the ball, the powder would be 'wiped off' and provide instant visual feedback of the contact point (see Figure 8.3). Paul got Thomas to hit a few shots and asked Thomas to look where he had impacted the ball. All the contacts were near the centre of the face. 'The fact that the contact is high on the club face is why you are not getting any height on your shots', Paul said. He asked him where he thought he should be making contact and Thomas said he needed to try and 'hit it lower on the club face'. Paul agreed and set the task of only hitting the bottom three grooves of the wedge, Thomas would know if he had been successful because of the visual feedback provided by the foot spray. Thomas hit a few shots, exploring different solutions and checking where he hit the ball on the face each time. Initially, Thomas struggled to hit the bottom three grooves, often hitting too low on the face and when he tried to correct, he went back to being too high. However, after a while he began to consistently hit the ball in the right spot and in doing so was producing a more consistent outcome with ball flight having a much steeper trajectory than with his old technique. Notably, Thomas reported that he was beginning to feel that he couldn't hit a 'fat' shot with these new dynamics. Paul probed Thomas again 'what does that feel like' Thomas said, 'It feels like I am slightly thinning it, it feels like I am clipping it off the turf'. Paul then asked: 'Did you do anything in the way you set-up to change this?' to which Thomas replied, 'Yeah I moved the ball forward in my stance'. Paul probed again: 'Anything else feel different?' 'Yes' replied Thomas, 'it feels like in order to only hit the bottom three grooves that my right hand is more active in the downswing and that when I finish the shot my hands more towards the left pocket of my trousers'.

In setting up the task in this manner Paul was keen to give Thomas a more external focus of attention (knowing that if he got too technical with Thomas it would be counter-productive). Paul wanted 'the task' to build the new action a more external focus of attention. The concept of allowing the task to build the action and using an external informational constraint

Figure 8.3 The use of foot powder on the club face can give a golfer instant feedback on the contact point made with the ball. The figure shows (left) too high, (centre) just right and (right) too low.

(i.e. the foot powder) to support the emergence of a re-organised co-ordination pattern are core principles of Paul's approach when he applies the CLA – essentially, he was affording Thomas the opportunity to self-organise a more functional way of controlling these shots.

Designing a CLA session to develop pitching skills

After assessing the current landscape of Thomas' golf performance, Paul focussed on the area where he thought he could make the most difference to Thomas' scoring. That is, the area of his game, which was the greatest rate limiter to improved performance, which he judged to be pitching. Paul used the GROW model to summarise the key features of the golf lesson (see Figure 8.4).

After identifying the goals for the session, Paul considered the reality and options to shape the Way Forward. He decided to add in a task constraint of using foot spray on the face of the club to encourage Thomas to strike the ball more consistently, lower on the face, and in doing so shallow the angle of attack into the ball. Paul also wanted every shot to matter, so rather than just pitching aimlessly to focus on 'technique', he set up targets placed around three different holes requiring Thomas to hit different distances. This constraint was added to help Thomas develop control and awareness of swing length and speed to achieve specific task goals. Figure 8.5 shows the set up for one ball position to hit to three pin positions. Finally, Paul outlined how he would set up the practice environment and how he would prepare Thomas for the session.

Selecting the practice environment

Using the environment selector, Paul's focus on pitching resulted in him choosing to use the short game area. This environment allowed him to spend as much time as possible 'pitching' as well as provided an environment that was representative of the course. This decision also allowed him to utilise the bunkers to increase the level of challenge by asking Thomas to pitch over them in Task 3 in an attempt to manipulate his emotions during practice.

Choosing the constraints to afford

Paul used the constraint builder to select the constraints he wanted to use to 'invite' Thomas to develop a more functional pitching technique. To do this, he chose a mixture of individual, environmental, task constraints. As discussed in the GROW section, Paul's choice of the short game area enabled him to replicate the actual environment of the course and also the opportunity to manipulate emotions by requiring Thomas to hit over bunkers. He also chose to add in a task constraint of a foot spray on the clubface. To ensure the practice task had a purpose and consequence, Paul set up a target zone around three flagsticks placed at different distances to design-in variability in hitting distances. The target zones enabled Thomas to get instant feedback on the accuracy of his performance.

PLANNING

G GOAL	R REALITY	O OPTION	W WAY FORWARD
• **What's the goal/ intention for this session?** To stop topping the ball when pitching • **How does this link to the overall goal?** To improve the ability to get up and down when missing the green • **The focus for learning is . . .?** Developing consistent contact when pitching from tight lies	• **What's the current skill level?** ○ Co-ordination? ○ Adaptability • **What affordances of the performance environment do you want to design-in to practice?** ○ Hard and soft surfaces ○ Hazards • **Which?** Hard surface/Hazards • **Why?** To invite adaptability • **When?** Task 2 & 3	• **What PRACTICE TASKS will bridge the gap?** Chipping from the edge of the green • **Which PRACTICE ENVIRONMENT will you choose from the environment selector?** Short Game Area • **What CONSTRAINTS from the CONSTRAINT BUILDER will you use and how will you manipulate them?** Hard surface, foot power, different hitting distance and an adjustable target zone- hazards • **How will you measure performance?** Number of balls in target areas • **We will know we have been successful if –** ○ **We can see** . . . more consistent contact with the bottom of the ball ○ **The data shows** . . . an increase in balls in target area ○ **The coach says** . . . the swing path is steeper ○ **The athlete feels** . . . more confident about making good contacts	• **How do you prepare the environment?** ○ 10 × 3 ball barriers around the fringe. ○ Cone circle initially at 1m (3 holes). • **How do you prepare the athlete[s]** ○ Explain why the ball needs to be hit from a steeper angle. ○ Describe the task. • **Anything else to be ready?** ○ No

PLANNING GUIDE

Figure 8.4 Using the GROW model to plan a pitching lesson.

Figure 8.5 This figure shows the set-up for one ball. To enable the task difficulty to be matched to emergent performance, the diameter of each target area can be reduced or increased by 30 cm after each set of 10 balls. If Thomas got 8/10 or more in the target zone, the zone diameter would be reduced by 30 cm, if he got 4/10 or less it would be increased by 30 cm. Any score of 5–7 would mean the target size would remain the same.

CONSTRAINT-LED SESSION PLANNING: ENVIRONMENT SELECTOR

VIRTUAL GOLF: INDOOR TRACKMAN		
BACKYARD: HITTING INTO A NET	SHORT GAME AREA	
PUTTING AREA ARTIFICIAL SURFACE		TURF
DRIVING RANGE ARTIFICIAL SURFACE		TURF
OFF-COURSE		

PAR THREE COURSES		
'A' COURSE	SIMILAR COURSE	"THE" COURSE
ON-COURSE		

← LEVEL OF REPRESENTATIVENESS OF LEARNING ENVIRONMENT →

Figure 8.6 The environment selector for golf.

THE CONSTRAINTS BUILDER FOR GOLF

INDIVIDUAL	ENVIRONMENT	TASK
Power	Surface Hardness	Competition Type
Fatigue	Grass Characteristics	Scoring System
Emotions	Wind	Competition Score
Intentions	Climate	Competition Position
Playing Style	Temperature	Clubs to Use
Confidence	Rain	Ball Types
	Green Speeds	Course Length
	Course Contours	Bunker Heights
	Course Location	Sand Type in Bunkers
	Club Culture	Additional Rules
	Opponents–Friendly	Mulligans
	Opponents–Aggressive	Reverse Mulligans
	Sledging	Speed Golf
	Caddies	Other Equipment —
		Barriers, Targets, Guides

Figure 8.7 The constraints builder for golf.

The session planner

Overview: once the previous sections had been completed, it was easy for Paul to fill in the detail on the session planner. The dials show how Paul manipulated representativeness of the practice task and variability. After initially providing a relatively low level in Task 1, variability was increased through to Task 3 with the intention of creating instability, by requiring Thomas to hit over bunker, potentially when quite nervous, with a commensurate impact on the swing. Task 4 was a repeat of Task 1.

Task 1: a pre-test. Paul set up Task 1 to provide a baseline of Thomas' current ability including qualitative and quantitative measures such as outcome and quality of ball contact. This task was completed without any additional constraints beyond randomly selected lies with balls dropped around the edge of the green requiring pitches of 10–20 m.

Task 2: in Task 2, Thomas was required to complete four sets of ten chips from the same ball positions, but this time was required to hit to three different pin positions and use the foot spray to gain augmented informational feedback on contact area. The target size would be adjusted depending on performance in line with the guidelines provided above.

Task 3: this is a repeat of Task 2, however, this time all ball positions will require Thomas to hit the ball over the bunkers surrounding the greens. The aim here is to increase the emotional intensity felt by Thomas to create greater realism in the practice and to deliberately design-in instability.

Task 4: the post-test. To evaluate the effectiveness of the session, Task 1 is repeated. The results would provide Paul and Thomas with the data

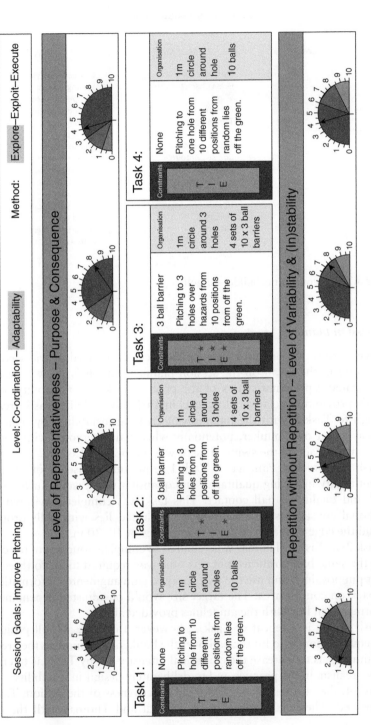

Figure 8.8 The session plan for golf chipping.

to inform the design of the next session. Consequently, the CLA session design process becomes cyclical with the next session emerging from the session before.

Summary

In this chapter we have brought to life the CLA for golf coaches. We highlighted the importance of golf coaches considering the performance environment as being just as important as the individual golfer in shaping skill during practice. We discussed the importance of capturing the client's history to enable the coach to frame what (s)he is seeing and how this background may be used to underpin the language used to get across sometimes complex golfing principles. By providing specific examples, we demonstrated how the coach can use a range of individual, environmental and task constraints in practice to create more representative learning environments and add variability to enhance skill adaptation during learning. Finally, using a case study example, we described how a golf coach used the CLA session designer to develop a specific lesson. Of course, in this brief chapter we have only touched the surface of how adopting a CLA may enhance the practice of golf coaches. We will build on these ideas in more detail in a forthcoming book in the series: *A Constraint-Led Approach to Golf Coaching*. This book will be co-authored with GPA professionals Peter Arnott and Graeme McDowell, who will provide the unique examples from their own work with golfers of all levels. We look forward to sharing our ideas with you there.

9 A constraints-led approach to coaching track and field

Introduction

The aim in this chapter is to demonstrate how the constraints-led approach (CLA) can be applied in the context of performance level track and field (T&F) athletics using specific examples from hurdles. Here, we draw on the experiences of Matt Wood, who is the Director of Coaching and lecturer in Sport Performance for Athletics at Cardiff Metropolitan University. Matt is also currently undertaking a professional doctorate examining non-linear pedagogy, utilising constraints-led methodologies in a track and field talent development environment. It is important to note that the case study and examples presented are an amalgam of various coaches and athletes and are not a representation of any one person. First, we consider some of the complexities of coaching T&F and, in contrast to the misconception that the CLA is purely a game centred approach (Harvey et al., 2018), show how the CLA can be applied just as effectively in individual sports. While much traction has been gained in the deployment of CLA in team sports due to the obvious issues of co-adaptation, chaos, complexity and self–organisation; the use of the CLA in individual sports is often questioned for legitimacy and this can result in coaches being more comfortable with the 'drill'-based approach to learning motor control and movement patterns in reputedly more 'closed' skill as they are supposedly 'repeatable' (but see Chapters 2, 3, 5 and 7, where we discuss the ideas of repetition without repetition that refute this idea). We offer a reflection on some key principles when coaching a sport like T&F using a CLA and refer to the GROW model as in previous chapters. In the next section we discuss some of the underpinning principles of a CLA approach in T&F, before describing a case study of an athlete, Natalie, outlining a CLA to coaching sprint hurdle starts.

Avoid thinking 'technical sports' can only be drill-based

Given its highly technical nature, the most prevalent approach to coaching hurdles has been to break the task down to optimise each sub-component using the design of coaching drills to elicit athlete development. For example, some coaches will prescribe take-off and landing distances for their hurdler, although individual differences in factors such as flexibility, agility, sprint capability and body size of each hurdler means there is no one-size-fits-all technical model for hurdling. In contrast to the prescriptive approach to coaching of technique, a CLA would promote a task simplification approach, and instead of directing athletes' attention on internal movement co-ordination, the focus would be on adaptation to the performance environment. This means that learning needs to occur with performance in mind (i.e. keeping the 'real' race in mind) and afford the learner the opportunity to develop a wide range of capacities required to succeed in a performance environment. For example, a key component in mastering hurdle technique is to bring the hurdle stride as close to the sprint stride as possible, allowing the athlete to 'run over' the hurdles without breaking stride to 'jump'. This can be very challenging for a novice or young hurdler, with the height and distance apart of each hurdle resulting in a focus of jumping over the hurdle rather than running over it. A coach who adopts a CLA would therefore match the task difficulty to individuals by simplifying the task and providing a range of reduced-height hurdles as well as different distances between the hurdles (Moy et al., 2014). A focus on learning to race by running over hurdles allows the coach to emphasise adaptation to environmental and task constraints. The contextual nature of performance is an important contributing factor to learning for athletes, and this should be considered just as prominently in individual sports as it is in team sports. For example, learning to hurdle in the rain, in windy conditions or on a wet surface, or simulating racing to qualify for a final, rather than a decontextualised focus on technique development. We provide a case study of Natalie in this chapter while also outlining other as examples of how we might utilise principles of a CLA in hurdles.

Principles of a CLA in track and field – more than just designing drills

While the ideas and concepts in ecological dynamics highlight that there is no one optimal model of executing a skill, there are a limited range of functional movement solutions due to the interaction between individual, task and environmental constraints. For example, fundamental biomechanical principles and structural constraints such as anatomy allied to the narrow task constraints associated with T&F events (e.g. the requirement to leave by the back of the circle in shot putting and discus, the specific weight and balance of the javelin or the requirement to take off behind a narrow take-off board in long and triple jumps) highlight that within each event, there are a number of signature positions or 'anchors' to which athletes pass through as the movement unfolds. We might refer to these positions as *fixed principles*. For example, in sprint hurdles, a fixed principle might include a specific body shape that the coach can recognise (i.e. it looks like hurdling) when going over the hurdles (i.e. staying low at the start, or positioning the landing leg for touchdown to decrease ground contact to maintain velocity through the take-off stride). In the case study later in this chapter, we show how keeping low and being fast through the first few steps may be important to consider when designing practices to improve the start, for a hurdler who is attempting to improve this part of their performance.

A key role of the coach in T&F constraints-led coaching is to ensure that the constraints employed encourage learners to 'find' these fixed principles. For example, for age group hurdlers, taking off from the 'right place' can be problematic as the distance between and height of hurdles changes as they move from one age group to the next. Consequently, in order to help a young athlete who is in transition between age groups and needs to re-calibrate his or her stride patterns to adapt to a new set of competition specifications, spatial markers such as cones can be placed before a hurdle (see Figure 9.1), to act as a guide for the learner, providing the opportunity to re-calibrate his or her actions and enable a take-off position that affords the athlete the opportunity to 'hit' the 'fixed position' when clearing the hurdle (i.e. the cones act as constraints to afford).

Purpose over process

A key requirement of adopting a CLA in T&F is to ensure that the primary goal or intentions of the practice task are not trumped by the constraints employed. T&F, similar to other sports, is susceptible to devices and gadgets that purport to be the magic bullet to enhance performance. It is therefore essential that any devices employed in practice must support the attainment of the primary goal. For example, if the goal is to increase a runner's speed, any constraint added should not act to significantly slow the athlete down, per se. For example, one task constraint widely used by coaches as well as strength and conditioning practitioners is 'Speed–Agility–Quickness' ladders. However, the movement patterns that are developed have been questioned by top coaches, who suggest they actually lead to lower knee lift and reduce stride length in attempts to increase cadence. Clearly, there is a need to better understand the fidelity of training practices to performance environments that move beyond the (purported) scientific analysis of physiological development and better understand how practices such as SAQ impact on skill adaptation and therefore performance outcomes.

External focus of attention

A key principle for the adoption of CLA in T&F is the use of an external focus of attention to help athlete's self-organise movements. For example, in hurdling, markers can be placed on the track (after the hurdle) to encourage the athlete to bring (coaches sometimes refer to this as the 'snap') his or her foot down quicker and therefore closer to the hurdle and ensuring that the

Figure 9.1 Constraining the penultimate step in hurdles to encourage finding 'fixed principles' in the movement regarding efficiency over the hurdles.

Figure 9.2 Without an informational constraint to provide opportunities for external focus of attention, here we see the hurdler perform a 'jump' over the hurdle rather than running over it.

horizontal breaking force is limited (a hurdler will need to land in an aligned vertical position), enabling the athlete to continue their running stride without a break in their momentum. Figures 9.2 to 9.4 illustrate how using an external marker can help a hurdler who is 'jumping' over the hurdle (Figure 9.2) to instead 'run' over it (Figures 9.3 to 9.4).

Throughout Figures 9.2 to 9.4 the use of constraints focuses on functionality and considers the principles of ecological dynamics and the constraints-led approach. In summary, CLA is an effective approach for T&F coaches who can apply the theory to practice underpinning their session design. In fact, in many ways, CLA is easier to use with individual sports as the only concern is to support the development of intra-individual–environment co-ordination, in contrast to team sports where inter-individual–environment co-ordination also needs consideration. To further demonstrate how CLA can be used in T&F, we describe the CLA session design process using the case study of Natalie, an up and coming talented 16-year-old athlete.

Case study – Natalie

The current landscape – knowing the athlete (session intention for Natalie)

Before deciding on the session intention, it is important to understand the current landscape for the performer(s). When collecting information about Natalie, the coach, Matt, needed to gather both qualitative and quantitative

Figure 9.3 With the introduction of markers on the floor, the athlete searches for this informational constraint and this can promote self-organisation to develop the stride pattern to 'run over' the hurdles.

information in order to develop learning and performance environments that elicit development. Natalie is a good national level athlete with international aspirations. Her current UK U20 ranking is top 30 for hurdles and high jump and top 25 for heptathlon. She is a senior champion for hurdles and high jump and is still only aged 16 years old. Natalie takes part in a few other sports (some team sports and individual sports) but is predominantly focussed on hurdling given that she shows a great deal of promise in this discipline. Matt is aware that the components that are key to Natalie, are speed (sprinting and a slight forward lean) and hurdle clearance time. Specifically, to keep the speed high and minimise flight time, Matt is keen to work with Natalie to understand her capabilities to perform (in terms of her take-off distance, clearance of hurdles and landing, etc.)

Specifically, Matt has identified that he needs to help improve Natalie's starts, something she is also aware of. When Matt first started coaching

Figure 9.4 The introduction of a tennis ball cut in half, and placed in the
landing pattern of this athlete provides an external focus for the
athlete to search for.

Natalie, he posed a number of questions when trying to understand her
performance history and aspirations (see Chapter 8 where we discuss the
importance of this in detail) and one key aspect was that her background in
other team sports meant that she had never really developed her race starts,
as often her speed was exhibited in games. Using video analysis of Natalie's
movement patterns and studying her aspirational split times (see Figure 9.6),
Matt was able to identify that Natalie was 'coming up too early' and needed
to stay lower to the ground for longer. In Figure 9.5 you can see that the
effect that coming up too early is having on Natalie's posture as her leg is
in front of her body and this stride length is causing her to create breaking
force in her running stride. The aim in a hurdle start is to 'set up' the first
hurdle clearance while running at optimal speed to be able to get into a good
rhythm when running over the hurdles. With regards to her 'start', Natalie
is trying to experiment with staying low for as long as possible giving her
sight of the first hurdle as well as generating the optimal speed she wants to
achieve for competitive racing times. Previous coaching interventions have left
Natalie feeling as though she is just focussed on the competition (e.g. going
from race-to-race) without having the specific developmental focuses she
needs to improve her overall goals. Consequently, this has resulted in Natalie
practising by focussing on 'running fast' and not on developing the required
running rhythm for hurdling that would result in her developing an appropriate stride pattern that enables her to take off from an optimal position at the
first hurdle. She has found in the past, that she is trying to run too fast (which
sounds counter-intuitive but there is a balance to strike with the technical

demands of the hurdles, and often the stride between hurdles is overlooked in development as athletes are encouraged to just sprint) and this often leaves her over-stepping with her landing leg, creating too much breaking force and foot contact time (which also brings about deceleration). Natalie is keen to develop and puts a lot of pressure on herself to sprint fast, but Matt has realised the need to work with Natalie on achieving a good balance between Natalie's body position (form) and speed. Matt and Natalie have worked together to agree on the body position that is to be achieved, and although this is, essentially, a qualitative judgment (feel, look, haptics and aesthetics), it is also measurable as Matt and Natalie have agreed some split times (Figure 9.6) to have some goals that are measurable in line with Natalie's aspiration to become one of the best athletes in the world. Consequently, Matt developed a session focussed on improving the start and worked with Natalie to focus on her acceleration and particularly on her body height during the first three or four steps of this phase. Figure 9.5 demonstrates the GROW model for planning these particular hurdles sessions.

GROW planning process

In the following section, a completed example of the four-step GROW planning process (Figure 9.5) is utilised to demonstrate the approach taken for the particular case study. After identifying the goals for the session, Matt considered the Reality and Options to shape the Way Forward. In line with his goal, he decided to add in a task constraint of a 150 cm high horizontal bar placed 120 m in front of the blocks. Natalie would therefore have to stay low by maintaining a more functional body position and keep her head down in the first few strides before 'coming up'. It also made her initially focus on getting through the barrier and delayed her focus from shifting to the first hurdle too early. Matt was also keen for Natalie to understand the importance of a fast start, without losing her rhythm and body shape over the hurdles so while they had an overall season goal in mind it was important to focus her body shape, which the constraint of introducing the bar is helpful for. Rather than her just giving her a general goal to run quicker though, Matt set the goal of reducing her current time to the first hurdle of 2.8 s to 2.5 s in line with the best times for her age group at the level of competition she is aspiring to reach.

What is the goal/intention for this session?

The goal of the session was to manipulate the forward lean in the acceleration/start phase of the hurdles.

How does this link to the overall goal?

The session will enable Natalie to develop a more explosive start by improving her 'pick-up' as well as enabling her to 'sight' the first hurdle.

G GOAL	R REALITY	O OPTION	W WAY FORWARD
• **What's the goal/ intention for this session?** Manipulating forward lean in acceleration/start	• **What's the current skill level?** Adaptation	• **What PRACTICE TASKS will bridge the gap?** Race starts under varying conditions	• **How do you prepare the environment?** Broom handle at start. Hurdles set for athlete stride length.
• **How does this link to the overall goal?** To improve the ability to 'pick up' the first hurdle after explosive start	• **What affordances of the performance environment do you want to design-in to practice?**	• **Which PRACTICE ENVIRONMENT will you choose from the ENVIRONMENT SEELECTOR?** Indoor Track	• **How do you prepare the athlete[s]?** Explain why looking down for first three strides is important. Describe task.
• **The focus for learning is . . .?** Not to be too upright too quickly	**Which?** Visual search for hurdle **Why?** Stay low for first three strides for explosiveness **When?** Start	• **What CONSTRAINTS from the CONSTRAINT BUILDER will you use and how will you manipulate them?** Task Constraint – Start under broom handle to keep low	• **Anything else to be ready?** No.
		• **How will you measure performance?** Speed of starts/success to first hurdle	
		• **We will know we have been successful if –**	
		○ **We can see** . . . confidence in start, not 'up' too early	
		○ **The data shows** . . . speed improved – improving time to hurdle by 0.1s to support progression through full race	
		○ **The coach says** . . . the athlete is getting over first hurdle in 2.3s	
		○ **The athlete feeds** . . .more confident into first hurdle	

PLANNING GUIDE

Figure 9.5 Using the GROW model to plan a hurdles session.

The focus for learning?

The focus on learning here was to understand that staying low allowed Natalie to get an explosive start to the hurdles as well as achieve rhythm and a balanced state so that she could run over the hurdles effectively. This also links to the impact of contact time (foot contact acts as a decelerating rate limiter) and the position over the hurdles (if an athlete is sprinting, as opposed to running at an optimal pace which is fast, but rhythmical).

What is the current skill level?

The current skill level was identified as being in the 'adaptability' level, as Natalie is already a high performing athlete.

What affordances of the performance environment do you want to design-in to the practice?

The aim of the training session was to develop a fast, rhythmical start, attuning to the first hurdle in order to get over it at running pace and with a good body position that doesn't slow Natalie down. The practice environment provided needed to include task constraints that would afford/invite the type of movement solution that Natalie needs to find.

Selecting the practice environment

Using the environment selector, Matt's focus on the sprint start resulted in him selecting a short indoor space in a hall. This environment allowed him to keep Natalie's focus on the start of the hurdles (in an outdoor space Natalie tends to want to just run the full 100 m as she likes the feel of a full race). The decision also allowed him to have a representative environment as the track surface is the same as Natalie's home race track, and while there was not enough space to run a full 100 m, Natalie was, in fact, able

Target	H 1	H 2	H 3	H 4	H 5	H 6	H 7	H 8	H 9	H 10	Finish
11.8	2.2	3.2	4.1	5.0	5.9	6.9	7.9	8.9	9.9	10.9	11.8
12.0	2.3	3.3	4.2	5.1	6.0	7.0	8.0	9.0	10.0	11.1	12.0
12.3	2.3	3.3	4.2	5.1	6.1	7.1	8.1	9.1	10.2	11.3	12.3
12.8	2.4	3.4	4.4	5.4	6.4	7.4	8.4	9.5	10.6	11.7	12.8
13.2	2.4	3.4	4.4	5.5	6.6	7.7	8.8	9.9	11.0	12.1	13.2
13.8	2.5	3.5	4.6	5.7	6.8	7.9	9.1	10.2	11.4	12.6	13.8
14.0	2.5	3.5	4.6	5.7	6.9	8.1	9.3	10.4	11.6	12.8	14.0
14.3	2.5	3.6	4.7	5.9	7.1	8.3	9.5	10.7	11.9	13.1	14.3
14.8	2.6	3.6	4.9	6.0	7.2	8.4	9.6	10.9	12.2	13.5	14.8
15.0	2.6	3.8	4.9	6.1	7.3	8.5	9.7	11.0	12.3	13.6	15.0

Women - 100m Hurdles

Figure 9.6 Ideal times for the sprint starts.

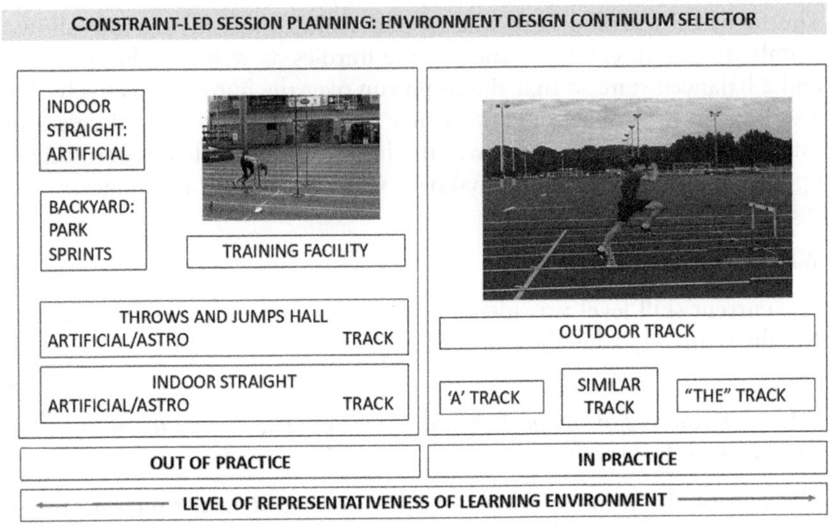

CONSTRAINT-LED SESSION PLANNING: ENVIRONMENT DESIGN CONTINUUM SELECTOR

| INDOOR STRAIGHT: ARTIFICIAL | | |
| BACKYARD: PARK SPRINTS | TRAINING FACILITY | |

THROWS AND JUMPS HALL			OUTDOOR TRACK		
ARTIFICIAL/ASTRO	TRACK				
INDOOR STRAIGHT			'A' TRACK	SIMILAR TRACK	"THE" TRACK
ARTIFICIAL/ASTRO	TRACK				

| OUT OF PRACTICE | IN PRACTICE |

← — — — LEVEL OF REPRESENTATIVENESS OF LEARNING ENVIRONMENT — — — →

Figure 9.7 The environment selector for hurdles.

to do more than simply practise her start and Matt expanded the practice to a four-hurdle start in order to afford Natalie the opportunity to 'feel like' the race and get a feel for how a good sprint start sets her up for the rest of the race.

Choosing the constraint to afford

Matt used the constraint builder to select the constraints he wanted to use to 'invite' Natalie to develop a more functional body position, one that would allow her to maintain eye contact with the floor at the start of the sprint, in order to stay low and visually attune to the first hurdle as she developed her optimal speed and rhythm into the first hurdle. To do this, Matt chose a mixture of individual, task and environmental constraints. As discussed in the earlier section, by selecting an environment where he was able to replicate the environment of the 'real' race, it afforded Matt the opportunity to direct Natalie's intentions towards running optimally but with rhythm and control. Matt chose to add in the task constraint of the bar as well as replicating the competitive nature of her event by asking Natalie to focus on times to the first hurdle and create competitive environments by getting her to focus on some of her favourite world class athletes and their times to the first hurdle. This use of a virtual competitor (i.e. a time constraint) allows Natalie to compare her progress with other elite performers.

Figure 9.8 Using a bar as a constraint to afford staying low to concentrate on the first three explosive steps.

We will know we've been successful if . . .

There is an improvement in the times that are recorded for the 'start' of the race. This is recorded by measuring the times to the various hurdles. We will see a rhythmical and balanced running style that is compact and does not show signs of deceleration. This can be measured by witnessing the placement of the landing foot in effective positions that allow for velocity to be maintained or improved through the hurdles.

The session planner

Overview: once the practice environments and constraints had been completed, it was easy for Matt to fill in the details of the session planner.

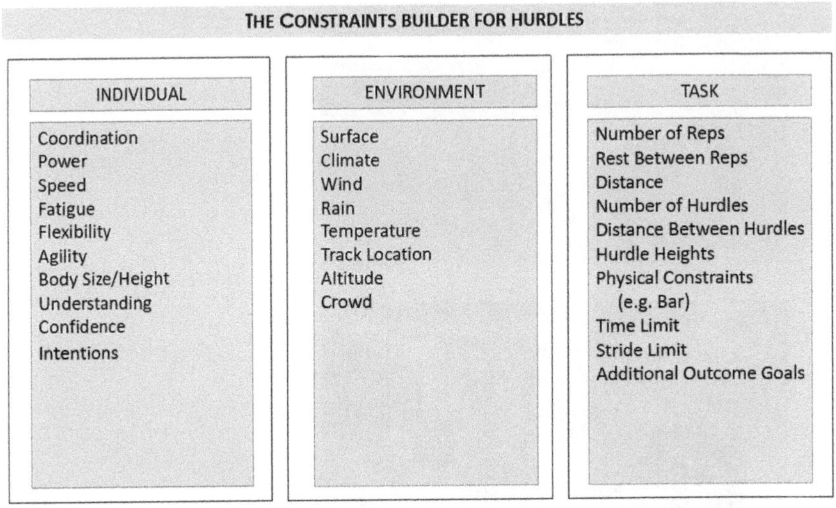

THE CONSTRAINTS BUILDER FOR HURDLES

INDIVIDUAL	ENVIRONMENT	TASK
Coordination	Surface	Number of Reps
Power	Climate	Rest Between Reps
Speed	Wind	Distance
Fatigue	Rain	Number of Hurdles
Flexibility	Temperature	Distance Between Hurdles
Agility	Track Location	Hurdle Heights
Body Size/Height	Altitude	Physical Constraints
Understanding	Crowd	(e.g. Bar)
Confidence		Time Limit
Intentions		Stride Limit
		Additional Outcome Goals

Figure 9.9 The constraints builder for hurdles.

The dials in Figure 9.10 show how Matt manipulated the purpose and consequence of the practice task. In particular, the dials show that Matt increased the level of representativeness (of a full race) from Task 1 to Task 2 by adding more hurdles to the practice. While he did not structure a full 100 m sprint, he did add four hurdles to stimulate more competition by providing Natalie with 'goal' times to meet for each hurdle. This is a key part of meeting the session intention as Natalie will only manage this time with a good body position. Matt supplemented this by manipulating the task constraints by changing the height of the bar. This constant adjustment was important in inviting Natalie to get into a good position and seeing the response of Natalie to self-organising and improving her sprint starts and improving her awareness for how she started best.

Task 1: a pre-test. Matt set up Task 1 to provide a baseline of Natalie's current 'start times' to the first hurdle as well as to video her form in order to get both qualitative and quantitative measures such as video analysis of her body shape and also the quantitative measure of time. This task was completed without any additional constraints. Matt simply asked Natalie to try different things to get a quicker start and see how that felt.

Task 2: in Task 2, Matt set up a bar (seen in Figure 9.11) to focus Natalie in order to stay low and get under the bar. He started by placing the bar at 150 cm so that Natalie had to organise into a strong and balanced position (seen in Figure 9.12). Matt then lowered it and adjusted it throughout the session to find the optimal affordance. Natalie and Matt discussed the height of the bar at the start of each 'sprint' and discussed the feeling at

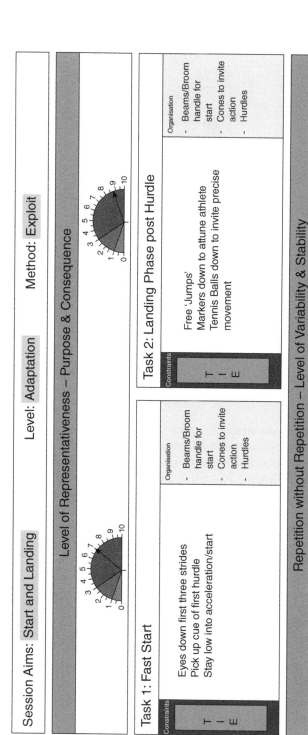

Session Aims: **Start and Landing**   Level: **Adaptation**   Method: **Exploit**

Level of Representativeness – Purpose & Consequence

Task 1: Fast Start

Constraints

T
I
E

Eyes down first three strides
Pick up cue of first hurdle
Stay low into acceleration/start

Organisation

- Beams/Broom handle for start
- Cones to invite action
- Hurdles

Task 2: Landing Phase post Hurdle

Constraints

T
I
E

Free 'Jumps'
Markers down to attune athlete
Tennis Balls down to invite precise movement

Organisation

- Beams/Broom handle for start
- Cones to invite action
- Hurdles

Repetition without Repetition – Level of Variability & Stability

Figure 9.10 The session plan for sprint starts in hurdles.

Figure 9.11 Athlete getting ready to start.

every point. They discussed the feeling of running under the bar. Did it feel different? Comfortable? Did she feel like it was aiding or hindering her start? Natalie had to attune to the information provided and in adapting to the environment stays low to produce the body position and movement required in accelerating through the first phase of the start.

Task 3: in Task 3 Natalie was required to 'race' through the first four hurdles while attempting to match or beat the competitive times of her favourite athletes as a 'virtual' opponent (e.g. a time constraint).

Session reflection

Matt used the bar to manipulate the forward lean in acceleration in order to improve Natalie's performance and functional movement. The bar therefore achieved Matt's key focus, which was to ensure that Natalie did not attempt to achieve an upright running posture too early in the run. The times that Natalie was successful, she was able to accelerate into her stride patterns and attune to the visual cue of the first hurdle, a key reference point for Natalie on race days. By staying low, and adapting her movement patterns to the bar, Natalie was able to produce greater acceleration. In order to stay low, she is encouraged to look at the ground and 'search' for the first hurdle only once she is through the bar. This is typical of hurdlers who will explode through the first few steps before searching for the visual cue of the first hurdle. While the race (and phases of the race) are practised, it is not as simple as always running the same number of strides, with the same power, explosion and height of the hurdle, and as such it is important to practise with representative and variable practice opportunities.

There are a number of nuanced and complex challenges that we have come across in developing a session that utilises a CLA in hurdles. Do the cones over-constrain? Is it really an affordance to run under a bar? In using the GROW model approach to design a constraints-led session, it is helpful when reviewing a session. The intention was to try to help

Figure 9.12 Going under the bar and accelerating through the first phase.

Natalie stay low and increase her pace through the first three-step phase. In staying lower, and not lifting her head to visually focussing on the first hurdle until she had passed through the bar, she is able to focus on her pace through the start. In reflecting on the session, we can identify that there are some issues with using constraints and 'getting it right'. Much of this is to do with knowing your athlete as we have discussed at length in previous chapters. We must respect the athlete's relationship with a performance environment. When trying to build constraints into session design it is important to recognize key sources of environmental information that underpin the functionality of an athlete's relationship with that environment in adapting actions to meet the problem faced. This is a key task for coaches and practitioners. In this particular session there are some fixed principles that are important. Using the bar as a task constraint, we are able to afford Natalie the opportunity to act by staying low, looking at the ground before raising her head to attune to the first hurdle and therefore act on the invitation (distance to the first hurdle means the athlete will coordinate and adapt their stride length to meet that first challenge). The use of the bar meant that the session intention was met as it was clear that Natalie was able to maintain pace and adapt her movement solution to the constraint. The invitation to act is implicit in the design of the learning environment and can also be explicitly guided by the coach by inviting the athlete to attune to the need to stay low and produce acceleration in the first phase of the race. These external foci lead to greater learning opportunities. Finally, it is important to consider individual differences, in so much as we need to assess constantly the physical, psychological, technical, strategic and emotional parameters of an athlete in order to meet the needs of the learner.

Summary

In this chapter we utilised a case study to demonstrate the use of the CLA for individual, technical sports. The examples from hurdles were used to show how the CLA can be used in an individual discipline like track and field and that, as coaches, we should not be afraid to explore the affordances in convergent sports in the same way we do in divergent sports. Utilising some guiding principles (Here we spoke about *Purpose over Process* and *External Focus of Attention*) to guide how we design constraints-led environments, we can support athletes at the performance level to explore the landscape of affordances available to them in order to invite action in convergent sports in a similar way to those of team sports, but with greater emphasis on the freezing and unfreezing of degrees of freedom in order to elicit the control of variability and instability in coaching. We have provided brief examples of how a CLA could enhance the practice of athletics coaches. We will build on these ideas in more detail in a forthcoming book in the series: *A Constraint-Led Approach to Track and Field Coaching*. This book will be jointly written by ourselves and international athletics coaches and movement science specialists from Physical Preparation backgrounds (S&C / EIS) coaches who will provide the unique examples from their own work with performance and development athletes. We look forward to sharing and discussing further ideas with you there.

10 A constraints-led approach
Conclusion

This foundational textbook summarised the key theoretical ideas that underpin a constraints-led methodology for sports pedagogy principles for designing learning environments for athletes, considered as nonlinear dynamical systems, in individual and team sports. Our aim in this book was to summarise current understanding of key ideas from ecological psychology, dynamical systems theory, evolutionary biology and the complexity sciences, which might inform the work of coaches, teachers and sport scientists in seeking to understand performance, learning design and the development of expertise and talent in different sports. In later chapters of the book we attempted to illustrate how practitioners might use a constraints-led methodology to achieve their practical goals. The book sets the scene for more detailed descriptions in the series that exemplify how practitioners use the methodologies of the constraints-led approach in a nuanced way to prepare athletes for performance, elicit skill and improvements during training and develop talent in individuals.

Some important messages emerged in the book that are worth re-emphasising in this concluding chapter for readers to act as a bridge for us to negotiate in the link to the forthcoming book series. Here we summarise some of the main, take-home messages:

1 The ecological dynamics rationale is really worth understanding in all its detail for sports practitioners to gain the most that they can from using the constraints-led methodologies and the nonlinear pedagogy approach in sport. A thorough understanding of key theoretical ideas and concepts would lead to a more nuanced application of constraints-led methodologies in sport performance preparation and practice. The four principles developed in this book provide a framework to apply key ideas of ecological dynamics. This is an initial and important attempt to help practitioners apply key theoretical ideas to their work using a constraints-led methodology. The framework allows sports practitioners to be more systematic and thorough in their consideration of the key features of this approach.

2 A provocative point to emerge in the book is that perhaps sports practitioners should consider themselves to be 'learning designers', regardless

of whether they work at a sub-elite, developmental or elite level. The descriptor of *learning designer* emphasises that athletes at all levels are still on a learning journey, albeit at different parts of the expertise trajectory. The term learning designer also places an emphasis on the importance of harnessing task and environmental constraints by helping each individual athlete to explore landscapes of affordances to utilise relevant opportunities for action. These ideas fit well with the chapter in this book summarising the role of the coach as an environment designer. Sports practitioners are architects of a learning experience.

3   Related to the message above, the pedagogical principles behind a constraints-led methodology has relevance for use with athletes of all abilities (able-bodied and those with disabilities), as well as children, adults (sub-elite and elite) and elderly individuals (at master's level performance).

4   The foundational text, taken together with the book series, shows the relevance of the constraints-led methodologies for designing learning opportunities for athletes in different sports and physical activities, regardless of the specificities of each performance environment. The key underlying principles, addressed in the initial chapters, remain the same regardless of whether the athlete is engaged in an individual sport like open water swimming, ice climbing, springboard diving or parkour, or is performing as part of a team, such as in relay events of running, cycling and swimming, and ball sports.

5   Sport practitioners should avoid stereotyping the language of constraints with negative connotations (that may exist in everyday communication). It's worth re-iterating here that the term *constraints*, used in this book series, has a special meaning in applied science, generally referring to a source of information (related to personal characteristics, tasks and environmental features) that can be used to regulate behaviours in performance and practice. Adopting a neutral interpretation of the concept of *constraints*, as information that regulates athlete behaviours, will help sport practitioners appreciate the subtlety and nuance needed in getting the most out of applying this methodology in performance preparation and practice. Related to a nuanced appreciation, application of constraints in learning tasks should not be viewed as a magic bullet that will automatically lead to intensive learning. Poor application of a CLA and ineffective learning designs are no better in enhancing learning than poorly conceived traditional practices that advocate constant repetitions and movement reproduction for all individuals. Under-constraining and over-constraining practice tasks are problems that can be avoided with more knowledge, understanding and experience as sport practitioners.

6   In this book and the ensuing book series, a key message is: know the athlete. Movement organisation in athletes and teams has a history. This is important to understand since it should shape the interactions a coach has with his/her athletes. This point is highlighted by the work of Pete Arnott in Chapter 8, who spends significant time 'interrogating

the athlete to understand why movements are the way they are'. This information is relevant to the language used by a sports practitioner. It also highlights why there is no one optimal solution to a performance problem. History reveals itself in the performance solutions that emerge from a learner.

7   Sport practitioners need to be mindful of the importance of intentions to frame a practice task. Understanding how to influence the 'intentionality' of an athlete during training (for example, in the sport of ice climbing, designing a scenario for climbers to ascend a surface quickly or securely), provides a relevant purposefulness to training, which reveals an obvious focus on process during performance and not just the mechanical achievement of outcomes. Furthermore, in team games practice, infusing a practice task with intentionality leaves no room for players to simply go through the motions in the small-sided practice games. Intentions can be used to shape the representativeness of learning designs and emphasises the need to consider the relationship between purpose and consequences in task design. Of course, this emphasis on intentionality helps athletes and sport practitioners explore links to the interactions of cognition, perceptions and actions.

8   Representative learning design (RLD) does not signify that sport practitioners have to design practice tasks that incorporate all features of competitive performance all the time. It is a fundamental misconception of a nonlinear pedagogy that successful application of constraints involves learning under full competitive performance conditions all the time. Of course, learning can occur during competition. But an important challenge for sport practitioners is to understand how to design representative learning environments, by manipulating task constraints, that each learner needs at that moment in his/her development. The new RLD dial built into the session planner provides a framework to deliberately consider how much RLD sport practitioners and athletes are seeking to co-create. For example, use of the dial encourages sport practitioners to consider how much variability is appropriate for learners to explore in a particular practice context in order to enhance adaptive behaviours. Such a perspective allows learners to exploit inherent self-organisation tendencies under constraints as a design feature. Task simplification is an appropriate method when designing practice tasks, for example, at the beginner level. Conversely, more experienced athletes may need to practise in highly specific practice environments as much as possible, since attunement to key information sources and key affordances is absolutely necessary. For example, if a baseball short stop needs to throw a runner out, that runner needs to be present in practice.

Over the past two decades an important contribution of the constraints-led research has been to enhance understanding of theory and application in the acquisition of skill and expertise in sport. This is an ongoing focus for sport practitioners to develop their understanding of how to get the best out of the rich methodological landscape that comprises the constraints-led approach to sport pedagogy. The challenge for contributors in the ensuing book series is to communicate in an engaging and meaningful way how sport practitioners may use the rich framework of the constraints-led approach to enhance the quality of practice in developmental and elite sport programmes. The book series provides an opportunity for us to engage more deeply with the evidence-based practice and the experiential knowledge of skilled practitioners involved with elite and developmental sport performance programmes.

The book series represents an exciting opportunity to explore the excellence in innovation and creativity of skilled and knowledgeable practitioners using constraints-led, sport practice and training programmes around the world. The book series seeks to give a voice to those practitioners who are willing to share their evidence-based practice in order to improve the quality of practical and applied work in sport from recreational, through developmental, to elite performance levels. An additional goal of this book series is to support the development of nonlinear pedagogy through the provision of practical exemplars that will enable readers to understand how the key principles underpin current practice in a variety of sports. It is worth noting that readers can gain a lot from learning how a constraints-led approach has been applied in different sports, which may or may not be related to their own area of sport expertise. It is the knowledge and skill in applying the constraints-led methodologies in a nuanced manner, regardless of specific context, and the implications of understanding the athlete and collective as an inherently nonlinear, complex adaptive system, which will yield rich insights for sport practitioners, seeking to become the best that they can. We take the opportunity to thank the book series contributors again for sharing their knowledge and understanding. There may be differences of opinion in how constraints manipulations are organised and applied. There are likely to be suggestions for how to modify practice task designs. That is to be expected because the theoretical rationale and the practical applications and utility of the constraints-led approach to skill acquisition, performance preparation and talent development will likely change, be updated and revised. The take-home message here is that sport practitioners need to perceive themselves as critical consumers, exploring and searching for solutions, asking questions, and facing challenges in the use of constraints-led methodologies. Sport practitioners, like athletes, should be ready to search, explore and exploit information and solutions in the quest to be the best that they can be. In this respect our area of applied science and practice should be viewed as a truly dynamic system.

Resources

Design your own environment selector

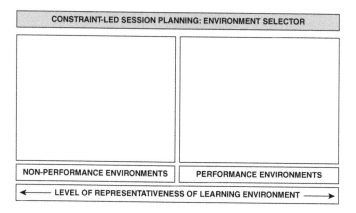

Figure R.1 Environment selector.

Design your own constraint builder

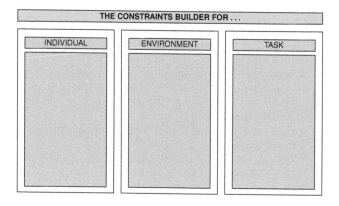

Figure R.2 Constraint builder.

References

Araújo, D., Davids, K., Chow, J.-Y., & Passos, P. (2009). The development of decision making skill in sport: An ecological dynamics perspective. In: Araújo, D., Ripoll, H., & Raab, M. (eds), *Perspectives on cognition and action in sport*, New York: Nova Science Publishers, pp. 157–169.

Araújo, D., & Davids, K. (2011a). Talent development: From possessing gifts, to functional environmental interactions. *Talent Development and Excellence*, 3, 23–26.

Araújo, D., & Davids, K. (2011b). What exactly is *acquired* during skill acquisition? *Journal of Consciousness Studies*, 18, 7–23.

Barris, S., Farrow, D., & Davids, K. (2014). Increasing functional variability in the preparatory phase of the takeoff improves elite springboard diving performance. *Research Quarterly for Exercise and Sport*, 85(1), 97–106.

Bernstein, A. (1967). *The coordination and regulation of movements*. London: Pergamon Press.

Boschker M. S. J., Bakker, F. C., & Michaels, C. F. (2002). Memory for the functional characteristics of climbing walls: Perceiving affordances. *Journal of Motor Behavior*, 34, 25–36.

Bowes, I., & Jones, R. L. (2006). Working at the edge of chaos: Understanding coaching as a complex, interpersonal system. *The Sport Psychologist*, 20(2), 235–245.

Brisson, T. A., & Alain, C. (1996). Should common optimal movement patterns be identified as the criterion to be achieved? *Journal of Motor Behavior*, 28(3), 211–223.

Bruineberg, J., & Rietveld, E. (2014). Self-organization, free energy minimization, and optimal grip on a field of affordances. *Frontiers in Human Neuroscience*, 8, 599.

Brunswik, E. (1955). Representative design and probabilistic theory in a functional psychology. *Psychological Review*, 62(3), 193.

Brunswik, E. (1956). *Perception and the representative design of psychological experiments*. Berkeley, CA: University of California Press.

Bunker, D., & Thorpe, R. (1982). A model for the teaching of games in secondary schools. *Bulletin of Physical Education*, 18(1), 5–8.

Burnie, L., Barrett, P., Davids, K., Stone, J., Worsfold, P., & Wheat, J. (2018). Coaches' philosophies on the transfer of strength training to elite sports performance. *International Journal of Sports Science and Coaching*. https://doi.org/10.1177/1747954117747131.

Button, C., Davids, K., & Schöllhorn, W. (2006). Coordination profiling of movement systems. In: Davids, K., Bennett, S., & Newell, K. (eds), *Movement system variability*, Champaign, IL: Human Kinetics, pp. 133–152.

Chemero, A. (2003). An outline of a theory of affordances. *Ecological psychology*, 15(2), 181–195.

Chow, J. Y., Davids, K., Hristovski, R., Araújo, D., & Passos, P. (2011). Nonlinear pedagogy: Learning design for self-organizing neurobiological systems. *New Ideas in Psychology*, 29(2), 189–200.

Chow, J.-Y., Davids, K., Button, C., & Renshaw, I. (2016). *Nonlinear pedagogy in skill acquisition: An introduction*. London: Routledge.

Davids, K., & Araújo, D. (2010). The concept of 'organismic asymmetry' in sport science. *Journal of Science and Medicine in Sport*, 13(6), 633–640.

Davids, K., Araújo, D., Correia, V., & Vilar, L. (2013). How small-sided and conditioned games enhance acquisition of movement and decision-making skills. *Exercise and Sport Sciences Reviews*, 41(3), 154–161.

Davids, K., Araújo, D., & Brymer, E. (2016). Designing affordances for health-enhancing physical activity and exercise in sedentary individuals. *Sports Medicine*, 46(7), 933–938.

Davids, K., Bennett, S., & Newell, K. M. (2006). *Movement system variability*. Champaign, IL: Human Kinetics.

Davids, K., Button, C., & Bennett, S. J. (2008). *Dynamics of skill acquisition: A constraints-led perspective*. Champaign, IL: Human Kinetics.

Davids, K., Glazier, P., Araújo, D., & Bartlett, R. (2003). Movement systems as dynamical systems. *Sports Medicine*, 33(4), 245–260.

Davids, K., Gullich, A., Shuttleworth, R., & Araújo, D. (2017). Understanding environmental and task constraints on talent development: Analysis of micro-structure of practice and macro-structure of development histories. In: Baker, J., Cobley, S., Schorer, J., & W., Nick (eds), *Routledge handbook of talent identification and development in sport*, Abingdon, UK: Routledge, pp. 192–206.

Davids, K., Handford, C., & Williams, M. (1994). The natural physical alternative to cognitive theories of motor behaviour: An invitation for interdisciplinary research in sports science? *Journal of Sports Sciences*, 12(6), 495–528.

Davids, K., Hristovski, R., Araújo, D., Balague-Serre, N., Button, C., & Passos, P. (eds) (2014). *Complex systems in sport*. London: Routledge.

Edelman, G. M., & Gally, J. A. (2001). Degeneracy and complexity in biological systems. *Proceedings of the National Academy of Sciences*, 98(24), 13763–13768.

Fajen, B. R., Riley, M. A., & Turvey, M. T. (2009). Information, affordances, and the control of action in sport. *International Journal of Sport Psychology*, 40(1), 79.

Fitts, P. M., and Posner, M. I. (1967). *Human performance*. Belmont, CA: Brooks/Cole.

Fitzpatrick, A., Davids, K., & Stone, J. A. (2017). Effects of Lawn Tennis Association mini tennis as task constraints on children's match-play characteristics. *Journal of Sports Sciences*, 35(22), 2204–2210.

Gray, R. (2018). Comparing cueing and constraints for increased launch angle in baseball batting. *Sport, Exercise, and Performing Psychology*, 7(3), 318–332.

Gibson, E. J. (1982). The concept of affordances in development: The renascence of functionalism. In: *The concept of development: The Minnesota symposia on child psychology* (Vol. 15), Hillsdale, NJ: Lawrence Erlbaum, pp. 55–81.

Gibson, E. J. (1988). Exploratory behavior in the development of perceiving, acting, and the acquiring of knowledge. *Annual Review of Psychology, 39*(1), 1–42.

Gibson, J. J. (1966). *The senses considered as perceptual systems.* Oxford, UK: Houghton Mifflin.

Gibson, J. J. (1967). New reasons for realism. *Synthese, 17*(1), 162–172.

Gibson, J. J. (1977). The theory of affordances. In: Shaw, R. & Bransford, J. (eds), *Perceiving, acting, and knowing: Toward an ecological psychology*, Hoboken, NJ: John Wiley & Sons, pp. 67–82.

Gibson, J. J. (1979/1986). *An ecological approach to visual perception.* Boston, MA: Houghton Mifflin.

Glazier, P. (2015). Towards a grand unified theory of sport performance. *Human Movement Science.* S0167-9457(15)30012-9. doi: *10.1016/j.humov.2015.08.001.* [Epub ahead of print].

Gorman, A. D., & Maloney, M. A. (2017). An applied example of the use of representative design in a team sport scenario. *The Brunswik Society Newsletter, 32,* 11–13

Greenwood, D., Davids, K., & Renshaw, I. (2012). How elite coaches' experiential knowledge might enhance empirical understanding of sport performance. *International Journal of Sports Science and Coaching, 7,* 411–422.

Greenwood, D., Davids, K., & Renshaw, I. (2014). Experiential knowledge of expert coaches can help identify informational constraints on performance of dynamic interceptive actions. *Journal of Sports Sciences, 32*(4), 328–335. Handford, C. (2006). Serving up variability and stability. In: Davids, K., Bennett, S., & Newell, K. M. (eds), *Movement system variability*, Champaign, IL: Human Kinetics, pp. 73–83.

Handford, C., Davids, K., Bennett, S., & Button, C. (1997). Skill acquisition in sport: Some applications of an evolving practice ecology. *Journal of Sports Sciences, 15,* 621–640.

Harvey, S., Pill, S., & Almond, L. (2018). Old wine in new bottles: a response to claims that teaching games for understanding was not developed as a theoretically based pedagogical framework. *Physical Education and Sport Pedagogy, 23*(2), 166–180.

Headrick, J., Davids, K., Renshaw, I., Araújo, D., Passos, P., & Fernandes, O. (2012). Proximity-to-goal as a constraint on patterns of behaviour in attacker-defender dyads in team games. *Journal of Sports Sciences, 30*(3), 247–253.

Headrick, J., Renshaw, I., Davids, K., Pinder, R. A., & Araújo, D. (2015). The dynamics of expertise acquisition in sport: The role of affective learning design. *Psychology of Sport and Exercise, 16,* 83–90.

Heft, H. (2003). Affordances, dynamic experience, and the challenge of reification. *Ecological Psychology, 15*(2), 149–180.

Hill-Haas, S. V., Dawson, B., Impellizzeri, F. M., & Coutts, A. J. (2011). Physiology of small-sided games training in football. *Sports Medicine, 41*(3), 199–220.

Hristovski, R., Davids, K., Araújo, D., & Button, C. (2006). How boxers decide to punch a target: Emergent behaviour in nonlinear dynamical movement systems. *Journal of Sports Science & Medicine, 5*(CSSI), 60.

Jacobs, D. M., & Michaels, C. F. (2007). Direct learning. *Ecological Psychology, 19*(4), 321–349.

Kelso, J. S. (1995). *Dynamic patterns, the self-organization of brain and behavior.* Boston, MA: MIT Press

Kiverstein, J., & Rietveld, E. (2015). The primacy of skilled intentionality: On Hutto & Satne's the natural origins of content. *Philosophia, 43*(3), 701–721.

Lee, M. C. Y., Chow, J. Y., Komar, J., Tan, C. W. K., & Button, C. (2014). Nonlinear pedagogy: An effective approach to cater for individual differences in learning a sports skill. *PloS one, 9*(8), e104744.

Liu, Y. T., Mayer-Kress, G., & Newell, K. M. (2006). Qualitative and quantitative change in the dynamics of motor learning. *Journal of Experimental Psychology: Human Perception and Performance, 32*(2), 380.

Magill, R. A., & Hall, K. G. (1990). A review of the contextual interference effect in motor skill acquisition. *Human Movement Science, 9*(3–5), 241–289.

Maloney, M. A., Renshaw, I., Headrick, J., Martin, D. T., & Farrow, D. (2018). Taekwondo fighting in training does not simulate the affective and cognitive demands of competition: Implications for behavior and transfer. *Frontiers in Psychology, 9*, 25.

Moy, B., Renshaw, I., & Davids, K. (2014). Overcoming acculturation: Physical education recruits' experiences of an alternative pedagogical approach to games teaching. *PE & Sport Pedagogy, 21*(4), 386–406.

Moy, B., Renshaw, I., Davids, K., & Brymer, E. (2015). The impact of nonlinear pedagogy on physical education teacher education students' intrinsic motivation. *PE & Sport Pedagogy.* doi: 10.1080/17408989.2015.1017455.

Müller, S., Abernethy, B., & Farrow, D. (2006). How do world-class cricket batsmen anticipate a bowler's intention? *The Quarterly Journal of Experimental Psychology, 59*(12), 2162–2186.

Newell, K. M. (1985). Coordination, control and skill. *Advances in Psychology, 27*, 295–317.

Newell, K. (1986). Constraints on the development of coordination. *Motor development in children: Aspects of coordination and control.* In: Wade, M. G., & Whiting, H. T. A. (eds), *Motor development in children: Aspects of coordination and control*, The Netherlands: Martinus Nijhoff, Dordrecht, pp. 341–360. http://dx.doi.org/10.1007/978-94-009-4460-2_19.

Newell, K. M. (1996). Change in movement and skill: Learning, retention, and transfer. In: Latash, Mark L., Turvey, Michael T., & Bernshteĭn, N. A. (eds), *Dexterity and its development*, Mahwah, NJ: L. Erlbaum Associates, pp. 393–429.

Newell, K. M., Moris, L. R., & Scully, D. M. (1985). Augmented information and the acquisition of skill in physical activity. *Exercise and Sport Sciences Reviews, 13*(1), 235–262.

Ometto, L., Vasconcellos, F. V., Cunha, F. A., Teoldo, I., Souza, C. R. B., Dutra, M. B., . . . & Davids, K. (2018). How manipulating task constraints in small-sided and conditioned games shapes emergence of individual and collective tactical behaviours in football: A systematic review. *International Journal of Sports Science & Coaching, 13*(6), 1200–1214.

Orth, D., Davids, K., & Seifert, L. (2018). Constraints representing a meta-stable régime facilitate exploration during practice and transfer of learning in a complex multi-articular task. *Human Movement Science, 57*, 291–302.

Orth, D., Davids, K., Araújo, D., Renshaw, I., & Passos, P. (2014). Effects of a defender on run-up velocity and ball speed when crossing a football. *European Journal of Sport Science, 14*(sup1), S316–S323.

Orth, D., Davids, K., & Seifert, L. (2016). Coordination in climbing: Effect of skill, practice and constraints manipulation. *Sports Medicine, 46*(2), 255–268.

Partington, M., & Cushion, C. (2013). An investigation of the practice activities and coaching behaviors of professional top-level youth soccer coaches. *Scandinavian Journal of Medicine & Science in Sports, 23*(3), 374–382.

Passos, P., Araújo, D., & Davids, K. (2013). Self-organization processes in field-invasion team sports. *Sports Medicine, 43*(1), 1–7.

Passos, P., Araújo, D., & Davids, K. (2016). Competitiveness and the process of co-adaptation in team sport performance. *Frontiers in Psychology, 7*, 1562.

Passos, P., Davids, K. & Chow, J.-Y. (eds) (2016). *Interpersonal coordination and performance in social systems*. London: Routledge.

Phillips, E., Davids, K., Renshaw, I., & Portus, M. (2010). Developmental trajectories of fast bowling experts in Australian cricket. *Talent Development and Excellence, 2*, 137–148.

Pinder, R., Davids, K., Renshaw, I., & Araújo, D. (2011). Representative learning design and functionality of research and practice in sport. *Journal of Sport and Exercise Psychology, 33*, 146–155.

Ranganathan, R., & Newell, K. M. (2013). Changing up the routine: Intervention-induced variability in motor learning. *Exercise and Sport Sciences Reviews, 41*(1), 64–70.

Reid, P., & Harvey, S. (2014). We're delivering game sense . . . aren't we? *Sports Coaching Review, 3*(1), 80–92.

Renshaw, I., & Chow, J-Y. (2018). A constraint-led approach to sport and physical education pedagogy, *PE & Sport Pedagogy*. doi: 10.1080/17408989.2018.1552676.

Renshaw, I., Chow, J. Y., Davids, K., & Button, C. (2015). *Nonlinear pedagogy in skill acquisition: An introduction*. London: Routledge.

Renshaw, I., Davids, K., & Savelsbergh, G. J. P. (eds) (2010). *Motor learning in practice: A constraints-led approach*. London: Routledge.

Renshaw, I., Davids, K., Phillips, E., & Kerhevé, H. (2012). *Developing talent in athletes as complex neurobiological systems*. In: Baker, J., Cobley, S., & Schorer, J. (eds), *Talent identification and development in sport: International perspectives*, London: Routledge, pp. 64–80.

Renshaw, I., & Fairweather, M. M. (2000). Cricket bowling deliveries and the discrimination ability of professional and amateur batters. *Journal of Sports Sciences, 18*, 951–957.

Renshaw, I., & Moy, B. (2018). A constraint-led approach to coaching and teaching games: Can going back to the future solve the 'they need the basics before they can play a game' argument? *Ágora para la Educación Física y el Deporte, 20*(1), 1–26.

Renshaw, I., Oldham, A. R., Davids, K., & Golds, T. (2007). Changing ecological constraints of practice alters coordination of dynamic interceptive actions. *European Journal of Sport Science, 7*(3), 157–167.

Rietveld, E., & Kiverstein, J. (2014). A rich landscape of affordances. *Ecological Psychology, 26*(4), 325–352.

Rosser, B. (2008). Econophysics and economic complexity. *Advances in Complex Systems, 11*(05), 745–760.

Rothwell, M., Davids, K., & Stone, J. (2018). Harnessing socio-cultural constraints on athlete development to create a form of life. *Journal of Expertise, 1*(1), 94–102.

Rothwell, M., Stone, J. A., Davids, K., & Wright, C. (2017). Development of expertise in elite and sub-elite British rugby league players: A comparison of practice experiences. *European Journal of Sport Science, 17*, 1252–1260. doi:10.1080/1 7461391.2017.1380708

Savelsbergh, G. J. P., Davids, K., Van der Kamp, J. & Bennett, S. J. (eds) (2003). *Development of movement co-ordination in children: Applications in the fields of ergonomics, health sciences and sport.* London: Routledge.

Schmidt, R. A., & Young, D. E. (1986). Transfer of movement control in motor skill learning. In: Cormier, S. M., & Hagman, J. D. (eds), *Transfer of learning,* Orlando, FL: Academic Press.

Seifert, L., Wattebled, L., Herault, R., Poizat, G., Adé, D., Gal-Petitfaux, N., & Davids, K. (2014). Neurobiological degeneracy and affordances detection support functional intra-individual variability of inter-limb coordination in complex discrete task. *PLoS One, 9*(2), e89865. doi:10.1371/journal.pone.0089865

Silva, P., Garganta, J., Araújo, D., Davids, K., & Aguiar, P. (2013). Shared knowledge or shared affordances? Insights from an ecological dynamics approach to team coordination in sports. *Sports Medicine, 43*(9), 765–772.

Simon, D. A., & Bjork, R. A. (2001). Metacognition in motor learning. *Journal of Experimental Psychology: Learning, Memory, and Cognition, 27*(4), 907.

Stoffregen, T. A., Bardy, B. G., Smart, L. J., & Pagulayan, R. J. (2003). On the nature and evaluation of fidelity in virtual environments. *Virtual and Adaptive Environments: Applications, Implications, and Human Performance Issues,* 111–128.

Thelen, E., & Smith, L. B. (1994). *MIT Press/Bradford book series in cognitive psychology.* Cambridge, MA: MIT Press.

Travassos, B., Araújo, D., Duarte, R., & McGarry, T. (2012). Spatiotemporal coordination behaviors in futsal (indoor football) are guided by informational game constraints. *Human Movement Science, 31*(4), 932–945.

Turvey, M. T. (1977). Preliminaries to a theory of action with reference to vision. *Perceiving, Acting and Knowing,* 211–265.

Turvey, M. T. (1990). Coordination. *American Psychologist, 45*(8), 938.

Uehara, L., Button, C., Falcous, M., & Davids, K. (2016). Contextualised skill acquisition research: A new framework to study the development of sport expertise. *Physical Education and Sport Pedagogy, 21*(2), 153–168.

Uehara, L., Button, C., Araújo, D., Renshaw, I., Davids, K., & Falcous, M. (2018). The role of informal, unstructured practice in developing football expertise: The case of Brazilian pelada. *Journal of Expertise/December, 1*(3).

Whitmore, J. (2017). (5th edition). *Coaching for performance: The principles and practice of coaching and leadership.* Great Britain: Nicholas Brealey Publishing.

Williams, A. M., Davids, K. & Williams, J. G. (1999). *Visual perception and action in sport.* London: E and FN Spon.

Withagen, R., Araújo, D., & de Poel, H. J. (2017). Inviting affordances and agency. *New Ideas in Psychology, 45,* 11–18.

Withagen, R., De Poel, H. J., Araújo, D., & Pepping, G. J. (2012). Affordances can invite behavior: Reconsidering the relationship between affordances and agency. *New Ideas in Psychology, 30*(2), 250–258.

Zelaznik, H. N. (2014). The past and future of motor learning and control: What is the proper level of description and analysis? *Kinesiology Review, 3,* 38–43.

Index

action capabilities 42
action-fidelity 78
adaptability 33–34, 46, 61, 65–67, 81, 89; and flexibility 32–33, 81; and stability 32, 41, 74
'adaptation + feedback' loop 44–45
affective learning design 79
affordances: in climbing 46, 59; continuum of 61; description of 4, 18–19 45–48, 54, 58–69; designing in 76, 86; in field hockey 109; a field of 32, 58–61, 160; as a niche 43; as opportunities for action 58; shared 57; in tennis 92
Arnott, P. 128, 161
athlete–environment relationship 18
attunement 14, 59, 76

behaviour: collective 51; functional 32, 39, 64, 78; emergent 16, 28, 49, 64, 74; goal directed 4, 15, 42–45, 79
Bernstein, N. A. 21, 26, 32–34, 51–54, 129
blocked practice: in golf 130
boxing 46, 63
Brunswik, E. 17, 21, 78
Button, C. 81

climbing: ice 59; rock 46, 60, 63
coaching: practice 9, 38, 67; methodologies 52
co-adaptation 49, 100: effective playing space 51; stretch index 51; team spread 51; synergy formation 41, 57
cognition 34, 44–45, 74–75; and emotions 42
complex adaptive systems: sports teams as 10, 26, 41; in nature 13–14
complex systems 13–14, 27, 82

conditioned coupling 48
constraints: to afford 76; in boxing 46; in cricket 23–24; description of 13–15, 42, 74; in individual sports 45–48; over/under constraining 160; in Rugby Union 53–54; scaling 54–55; sociocultural 16, 65–67; in springboard diving 48; systematic and unsystematic manipulation of 82; in team sports 48–55; in tennis 54
constraints builder: in field hockey 111; golf 139; track and field 154
constraints led-approach: definition of 43–44, 52, 73–82; case studies using GROW model in field hockey 105–126; in golf 126–137, 142; in track and field 142–159
coordination: in collective systems 28; definition of 89; of degrees of freedom 26–27; dynamics 27–28; patterns 15, 34, 38, 41, 48–51
cricket 36, 74; Merlin (bowling machine) 23–24, 79
Cushion, C. 109

Davids, K. 1, 16, 52, 59, 76, 90, 91, 102, 108, 126, 143
decision-making 45, 64
degeneracy 33
degrees of freedom 26–27, 31
dexterity 21, 32–33, 52–54, 113
dynamic instability 110
dynamical systems theory 14, 159

ecological dynamics 10, 17, 45, 74
ecological psychology 4
edge of chaos 83
emergent movement patterns 42